# PUBLIC PROJECTS

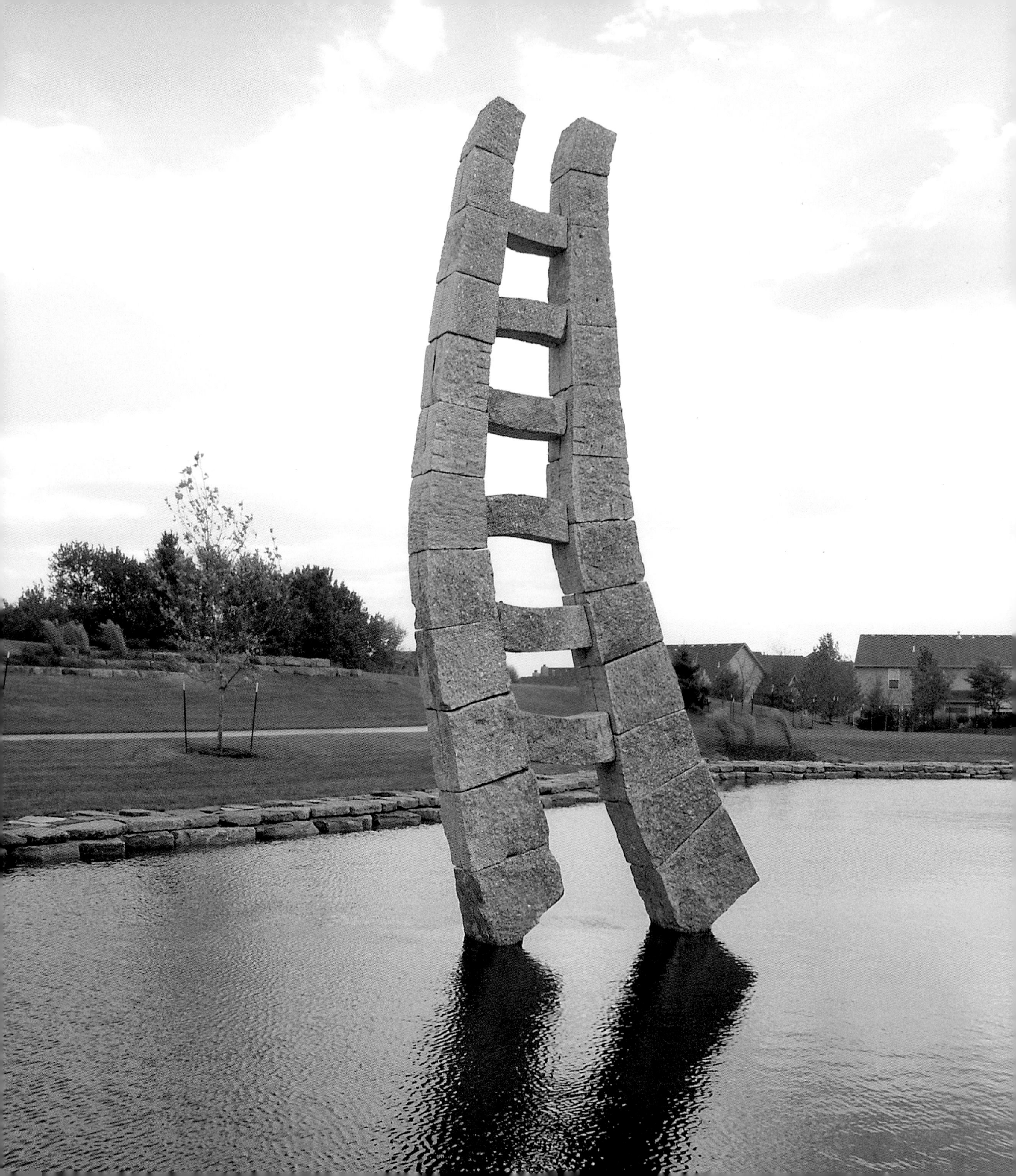

# ILAN AVERBUCH

## PUBLIC PROJECTS

CHARTA

Concept
Ilan Averbuch

Design
Mario Piazza, Letizia Abbate (46xy studio)

Editorial Coordination
Daniela Meda, Filomena Moscatelli

Copyediting
Emily Ligniti

Copywriting and Press Office
Silvia Palombi

US Editorial Director
Francesca Sorace

Promotion and Web
Monica D'Emidio

Distribution
Antonia De Besi

Administration
Grazia De Giosa

Warehouse and Outlet
Roberto Curiale

Cover
Reflection in water of *Avanim Vetseadim
(Steps and Stones)*, 2008,
Gezer Park, Leawood, Kansas

Back cover
*Avanim Vetseadim (Steps and Stones)*, 2008

Photo Credits
all photos by Ilan Averbuch except:
Jackie Baird, p. 41
Christophe Berney, pp. 30, 48, 54, 62, 90
Avraham Hai, p. 8
Dr. John Kenney p. 86 (upper picture)
Rachel Lazar, p. 43
Georges Lindenmeyer, p. 85
Jeffrey Sturges, p. 52
Chris Watson, pp. 25, 36, 56, 63
Yael Yaery, p. 20





Edizioni Charta srl
Milano
via della Moscova, 27 - 20121
Tel. +39-026598098/026598200
Fax +39-026598577
charta@chartaartbooks.it

Charta Books Ltd.
New York City
Tel. +1-313-406-8468
international@chartaartbooks.it
www.chartaartbooks.it

ACKNOWLEDGMENTS

Thanks to Christophe Berney, sometimes #2 and other
times #1, my closest friend, for all the knowledge he
has shared with me, from photography to computers,
to how to build and install my sculptures. Better
for actually traveling with me to build many of them
in remote places, and for sharing with me his great
appreciation of nature. That makes it all more alive.

To Todd McCollister, who is responsible for
my "upstairs world," where I conceive and compete
to execute my ideas, for all the wonderful work
in coordinating this book and preparing each and
every aspect of it, and of the public projects.

To José Morocho, for cutting the mountains of stones
and fabricating these works with me, without ever
being able to travel and see the work, nor his kids.

To Michael Moore, for editing my emotional writing
and putting sense in my stories.

To Nancy Hoffman, who has believed in me
and has shown my difficult work since 1989 in SoHo
and Chelsea, including many that became public
works. To Chris Watson at the Nancy Hoffman Gallery,
who installed, carried, photographed, and managed
my work in the gallery, as well as being a friend for all
these long years. To Sique Spence and Judith Nichols,
who were always there for me.

To Olga Korper, for daring to schlep the work
to Canada and show it in Toronto for so many years.

To Ruthi Ofek and Arieh Dahan for doing so much
for me in Israel, and above all Stef Wertheimer,
who conceived and created Tefen, which paved
the road to what followed.

To Lutz Teutloff for all the past years of supporting
and presenting my work in Germany and Canada.

To Rakhi Sarkar for enabling and supporting my
Calcutta endeavors.

To all the wonderful people that I met along the way
in the world of public art, who made it possible to have
the work built so far from home.

And last, to my wife Alka and my daughter Maya,
for growing up with me.

Ilan

# ILAN AVERBUCH:
## THE NEW PARADIGM OF PUBLIC SCULPTURE
### MARK DANIEL COHEN

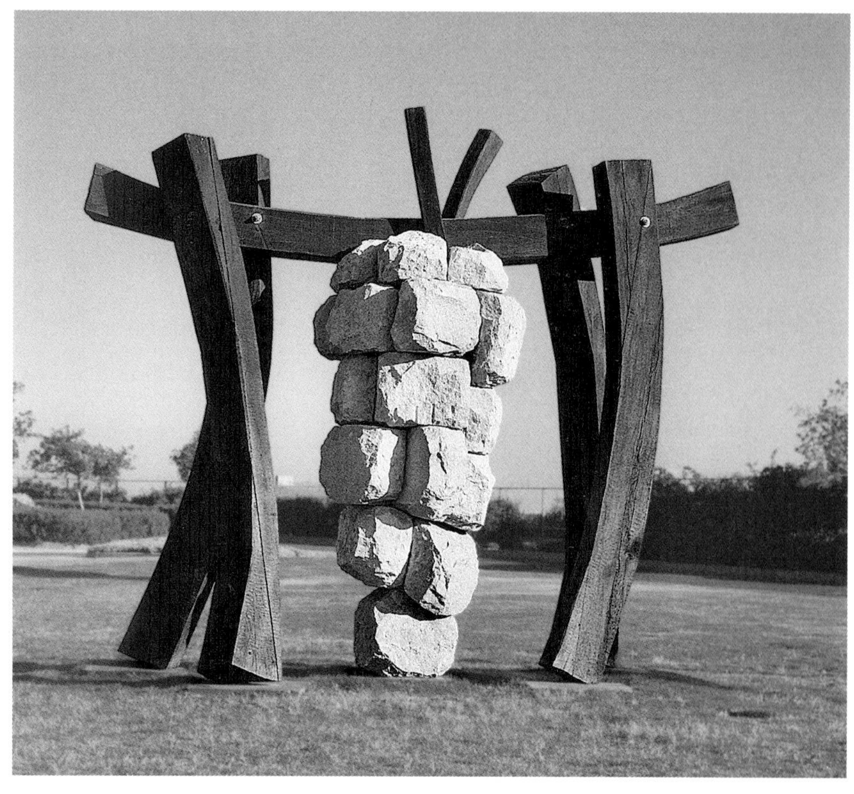

**Promises Promises**, 1994
Wood, stone
9 x 10 x 10 feet
The Open Museum, Tefen, Israel

There's a sense in which all sculpture is public art, and in which all public art is a form of sculpture, regardless of how it is made, regardless of the style it fashions. For of the visual arts, sculpture is the one art form that makes its passage back through the looking glass; it is the one that violates the separation between the aesthetic realm and our own; it is the one that departs its native territory of imaginative space and enters into our world, rather than requiring that, to meet it, we imaginatively disembark the here and now and make the move into its world. Sculpture is— or rather, the contents of a work of sculpture, the things and events depicted, the tale being told—physically real. A sculpture of a person is literally real in the very sense that a person is literally real. All the other visual arts depict, convey simulations, merely appear. But sculpture does not seem—it is.

Sculpture emerges. It enters the public sphere. And so sculpture is the art that has taken on public functions. It has borne social responsibilities. It is a social signifier— it gestures to a body of people, it marks moments of significance to them. We have used sculpture to celebrate our triumphs, to mourn our dead, to memorialize our losses, to sanctify our battlefields, to commemorate our ambitions, and perhaps above all, to assert our urge to monumentality, to testify our glory. The monuments that pock the passing of every civilization are acts of sculpture.

But ours is not a time for public commemorations—not in the traditional sense and not to the degree it has been done before us. We seem not to be so inclined as a social body—perhaps more to the point, we seem not to be so much a social body any longer. The unified spirit that underlies celebration of victory in war, memorializing of heroes in battle, recognition of our joint aspirations, our common tragedies, appears not to be among us any longer.

Sculpture and its inherency as our public art form of course continues, as art forms must and do, seeking in the works of the most prolific and imaginative practitioners new formulas, new principles of a renewed pertinence, new ways of recording, even creating, what is significant to their time. The project of seeking a new role for sculpture, a function to replace the purposes of commemoration and monumentality, can be said to have been in progress ever since Rodin, and in particular since his *Burghers of Calais*, a commemorative work of distinctly introverted gazes, a work of heroic acknowledgement not elevated and celebratory, but turned inward, away from the public realm.

In our time, the development of new formulas and fashions continues in the works of the most prolific and effective sculptors, and in the most overtly public work, there are few sculptors who are more present in the contemporary cultural environment than Ilan Averbuch. Over his thirty-year-long career, Averbuch has become one of our most successful public sculptors. His works appear over a great part of the globe, including India, Israel, Poland, Germany, Switzerland, Canada, and many parts of the United States.

And Averbuch is one of our most effective public sculptors in a sense far more significant—in the sense of pure aesthetics: he has developed a manner of sculpture, a style of conception and execution, that is distinctly his own, and that is distinctly suited to the nature of public projects, distinctly and deliberately suited to solving the conundrum of public projects done in a time of withdrawn public sentiment—the conundrum since the time of Rodin. In short, he has developed a new paradigm for public sculpture, a new model of public works tailored to our moment in history.

It is not merely that Averbuch works in forms and with materials that are unmistakably his own. There is that, but there is more: he works in a style, with a feeling of personal identity, that is his own. One can never mistake an Averbuch sculpture for that of anyone else, not merely because of its forms and combinations of forms, but for the fluid movement of thought, the personality, the character of dreaming, that laces through all his acts of creation. They do not merely look like no one else's; they feel like no one else's.

What Averbuch has achieved in his personal style, and what no other contemporary sculptor has done to anywhere near the same degree, is fuse together the visual linguistics of public presentation with the private imaginative formulations of pure aesthetic investigation. In a phrase, he creates public works that replace commemoration with rumination, with pure, free-roaming imaginative speculation, without sacrificing the public role each work plays. His sculptures are assertively personal exercises of creative thought, employing a set of idiomatic forms and symbols of his own devising, and yet they are not hermetic. At the same time as they are entirely personal, they are also highly and surprisingly accessible to the general viewer, as is evident from their popularity and the number of public commissions he continues to obtain. The sculptures are austere in their reserve, in the purity with which they speak Averbuch's private artistic vocabulary, and yet they are inviting to the viewer—actually, more than inviting, they are prepossessing. There is a rich, intellectually compelling component to his sculptures, and there is also a sense in which they are immediately and inescapably likable, which is no small thing for any artist.

In essence, what Averbuch has done is conduct the artist's private imaginative journey—the artist's inner journey—in the territory that the public sculptor had occupied for the sake of practicing public commemorative functions. He tells his personal story, the story of the journeys of his imagination, the story of his mind, in place of society's story. In a sense, he has pulled the Alice in Wonderland aesthetic realm even further back through the looking glass, back into our realm, than sculpture normally does. He has drawn the artist's mental sketchpad, the artist's exercises of sheer artistic dreaming, into our world, as physically real elements, as real as we are. Despite the fact that, by their scale and placement, Averbuch's public sculptures are monuments, there is something evidently intimate about them. The sculptor acknowledged as much in the title of a 2008 exhibition at the Nancy Hoffman Gallery in New York: *Ilan Averbuch: Intimate Monuments*. And he has noted that: "All my works are a dialogue between the intimate and the monumental. They are monumental, but with a question mark."

And yet it is not accurate to say that the public function of social cohesion has been replaced by the artist's private visual ruminations in Averbuch's works. These public sculptures of private vocabulary achieve both. They do the public sculptor's work—of integrating his creations with the already existing, surrounding environment, acknowledging, complementing, and reflecting it, even commemorating it in a sense, rather than imposing upon it. And at the same time, Averbuch's sculptures explore the personal concerns of the artist, concerns that turn out to address issues of social import, of public concern, issues such as political conflict, the possibilities of optimism, war, modernist aesthetics, the failure of the utopian ideal, and the impossibility of the monumental vision.

One becomes fluent in Averbuch's private artistic vocabulary, in the personally devised meanings of his forms, through gaining familiarity with his works. One learns their meanings, and their principles of meaning, by looking. The best place to begin is with a sculpture that, better than any other, powerfully and purely demonstrates the workings of his artistic vocabulary, and for that reason is ideally titled: his stunning and impeccably conceived *Self-Portrait* (2008).

Standing 12 feet high, *Self-Portrait* is a concise and inspired statement of the artist's methods and themes. The work is constructed out of panes of frosted glass arranged as a conic section, rising from a cylindrical metal base, fanning upwards like a tree and set in an enormous rectangular lead frame that stands off balance, one corner of the frame seeming to jut into the floor. The image within the frame is fragility set within hard substance, with the panes of glass, the fragments of glass, displaying the shadows of the metal armature that holds them in place, like a skeleton showing through the skin—the limpid, translucent delicacy of glass enclosed in and upheld by the endurance of metal. The work resembles a cameo conceived on a looming scale, but the portrait—the precious image that we traditionally display on walls and hold in lockets—would normally be set in a gold frame. Here, the fragile intimacy is undercut with a frame of lead, a gray, dull, and poisonous metal. It is a portrait of the artist— "Ilan" is Hebrew for "tree"—as conceived by the artist, and it is specifically the self-portrait of a sculptor. The image bursts its frame, literally cutting into and through the frame on one side—like all sculpture, it is public, it is physically real. Unlike painting, it extends beyond the protected space within the frame, extends into the world, into our space. And what extends is not just an abstracted organic image, a tree image, but is as much the form of a fountain, a geyser, an upward surging, of energy, of creative imagination, of the thrust and enthusiasm—the *élan*—of the creator: the creative vision, the sheer urgency to create, to make something real, rising like a fountain, breaking through its limits, becoming itself something real.

It is a private image, a personal, idiosyncratic visual expression of the artist contemplating, presenting, himself. Yet, in a related work, we can see a similar image functioning in the public sphere, doing the intricate work of contemporary public sculpture.

*Under the Shadow of a Big Tree* (2009) is a commemorative work, located in Tephford Park, in Tamarac, Florida. The composition is nearly the same, but has been altered in significant ways, to acknowledge knowingly the space it occupies and to pursue the public purpose of its creation. First, the materials have been changed. The fragile glass of the tree form in *Self-Portrait* has been replaced with stone here, to add the durability a public sculpture requires to exist in the world. The rectangular frame has now become an oval

one, to react to and establish a dynamic tension with the circular space in which the sculpture is placed. The frame that had been the cameo setting for his self-portrait is here a frame for views of the canal, the park, and the buildings in the surrounding area. Like many of Averbuch's public works, the sculpture serves as a gateway or an entry point that brings people into and integrates them with the surrounding environment. The tree form that in *Self-Portrait* had been the center of the artist's self image is here a clear reference to the tree of life, a commemoration in a place dedicated to Deputy Brian Tephford, a police officer who gave his life in the line of duty. A composition that in one work serves as a reference to the artist who created it—a completely private image—here serves as an acknowledgement of the death of another, of the other.

Among the most interesting and ingenious strategies for integrating his public sculpture into its environment are his works at railroad stations: at Tacoma, Washington, and Phoenix, Arizona. Both projects are constructed of two works, and are devised to reflect and respond to, not only the immediate environment, but the history of the place where they are installed, as if they naturally arose and at the same time deliberately responded to the identity of their geography.

At the South Tacoma Station, the project includes *South Tacoma* (2008) and *End of the Line* (2008). Tacoma's architecture is marked by the use of rolling arches—the original train station (now the U.S. Court House) has them, as does the history museum. In *South Tacoma*, situated at the north end of the station, Averbuch turned the form of the arches upside down to fashion two Corten steel wheels, similar to the steel wheels of railroad trains, as well as creating circular arches to serve as a gateway to the station. Each of the sculpture's wheels is crossed by a stone band that hovers in the air like railroad ties suspended upside down, above the earth, made light, ephemeral, dream-like, magical. Like the stone work in almost all of Averbuch's sculptures, the bands are made out of stones previously used, stones from old buildings in this case. Averbuch has said he finds recycled stones visually more interesting than new stone. He knows also that old stones root his works to the ground on which they are installed. They refer to the past of their place; they are literally built of it. The use of old stones is continued in *End of the Line*, a curving granite ribbon that is buried in the concrete train platform, runs the length of it, and leads visitors into the south entrance of the station. The end of the granite ribbon rises up out of the concrete and takes the form of a large hemispheric granite stone. Like the circular cut of the giant steel wheels, the curving rhythms of the granite ribbon are like the harmonic rhythms of train travel itself, and the granite stone hemisphere rising up is the end of the motion, the completion of the journey at the station.

The principal work in Phoenix, *Landmark (The Crossing)* (2008), employs a single, large circle, this time of stone. It is a gateway made of desert stones, an entry to the place. A complete circle, it reflects the light rail system at the station—a place where travel never completely ceases. And, reflective of the history of the place, like a gateway that passes us back in time, the circle refers to the Hopi Indian belief that life is a circle that each of us enters at a different point. Apparently stepping through the circle is a line of tall steel stanchions, each topped with a block of desert stone, perhaps a line of people passing the gate, perhaps those who once came to cultivate the land, perhaps stalks of grain being shipped out by rail.

*Landmark (The Crossing)* is complemented by a small work, *Trough, Seat, and Tree* (2008)—actually, two copies of the sculpture, one on the north platform, one on the south. The composition is of a line of granite stones, with a trough carved along the top of them, which intersects with a concrete seat, forming a corner that embraces a triangular planter, which holds vegetation and a large shade tree. At regular intervals, water flows through the trough, dripping close to the tree and watering the vegetation. More than a decorative work, the sculpture is a resting place for travelers, an oasis in the station.

The large, vertical circle is one of the recurring images in Averbuch's work, one of the enduring elements in his private sculptural vocabulary, and its immediate reference, its relation to the environment, constantly changes even as its symbolic meaning—its feeling of the cyclical continuity of existence—remains constant. In *Bridges and Reflections* (2001), situated in front of the performing arts center at Illinois Central College, Peoria, two 18-foot high stone circles are cut across the middle by a linear horizontal motion of steel elements—another of Averbuch's recurring visual themes: the hovering horizon line, suspended dreamily above the earth. Here, the line is the river, the movement of water, with the steel elements resembling a cityscape—reflecting Peoria as a city divided by a river, each half reflected in the water below.

The range of forms and sheer imaginative prowess Averbuch can bring to the demands of integrating his public sculpture into the landscape is illustrated with remarkable variety in his Portland, Oregon, project at the enormous Rose Garden, which includes an indoor sports arena and a coliseum. The Rose Garden is located across the river from the main area of Portland, with three approaches to the complex by way of three bridges. Averbuch created three sculptures to mark the three approaches, each work in a style unlike the other two, reflecting the nature of Portland as a one-time frontier town, which drew waves of immigration over the course of its development, involving the continuous integration of many distinct cultural groups and styles.

*Stone Water and Heaven* (1995) is like a large version of a garden sculpture, with a single seraphic copper wing rising next to a circle of stones, water in a circular trough cut along the top of the stones. *The Little Prince* (1995) is a gigantic fallen crown, an image of a ruin of ancient majesty, of one-time splendor, and a version of another recurring theme in Averbuch's work: the obsolescence of the monumental, former monuments in the soil, like ancient relics. *Terra Incognita* (1995) is an enormous gateway made of wood and stone. Seventeen feet high by 40 feet long, it is another of Averbuch's hovering horizontal lines, holding up two massive blocks of stones. Three enormous cords of vertical, pointed wooden stakes bolster the structure, one cord in the middle and one at each end, with open spaces below the stone blocks, like gateways through which the entering crowds could pass. The work is one of the purest examples of the distinguishing characteristics of Averbuch's sculpture: tied to the environment, idiosyncratic, and yet entirely accessible, its imagery impossible to completely misunderstand, even if ultimately mysterious and impossible to fully comprehend.

Even as Averbuch's private sculptural vocabulary ingeniously conducts the technical work of public sculpture, of integrating sculpture and the environment in a manner useful and meaningful to the public, it also continues the contemporary paradigm by conducting Averbuch's private artistic journey, as uniquely his own as that of any studio artist. The range of his themes, his artistic concerns, is large and far too extensive to be explored fully here—much of it can be seen in the images in this book. However, what may be considered his primary, most frequently recurring themes are worth examining briefly.

One of the most compelling concerns in Averbuch's oeuvre is the impossibility of the monumental. It is the "question mark" in his "monuments": the recognition that we no longer seem inclined to celebrate the place we hold in the cosmos and our endurance beyond the vicissitudes of history. Perhaps, it is because we have become too post-modern, too self-aware of ourselves as creatures of history, rather than seeing ourselves champions of its defeat. But to a greater extent, it is because of the century of disillusionments we have just suffered. The twentieth century was the great experiment in utopian visions, in efforts to end the continual drifting of civilization, to complete and perfect the human story—to achieve an "end to history." And we know now that it all came to naught.

In a series of works created over a period of more than twenty years, Averbuch's aesthetic concern has been with the aftermath of the disillusionment that has followed our utopian pursuits, that has come with the failure of our dreams. These sculptures seem to be post-apocalyptic, not in the sense of being visions that arise after the end of civilization, but visions that arise after the end of unqualified hope, after the belief in unlimited possibility. They are post-monumental works, which recognize that human history is little more than a struggle to survive, and human perfection can never be achieved.

Categorically, this is the theme of the fall, and it is carried through Averbuch's career by works with fallen elements. Most directly and in his earlier years, the frequently recurring image was a dome or a crown fallen to the earth. In *The Fall* (1989), *After the Reign* (1990), *Berlin Dome* (1994), *The Little Prince* (in the Portland project), and *She Wolf* (1995), the symbol is clearly one of fallen majesty: the gigantic form of a crown in the dust or of a toppled dome. The form of *She Wolf* transforms the fall of majesty into the image of war, for it also resembles a missile, a weapon of destruction, as well as the she wolf of the title—a clear reference to the legend of Romulus and Remus, sons of Mars, the god of war, who were raised by a she wolf and who became the founders of ancient Rome, and thus of civilization. Our grandeur, our glory, is nothing but the result of war, and like the empty interior of the sculpture that is revealed in the view from the back, it is a vacuous thing.

The fallen form takes on a new structure in later works, a structure of the broken vessel, as in *In the End of Utopia (The Big Balloon Is Far)* (1999), *Air* (1996), and *Time Passing* (1997). *In the End of Utopia (The Big Balloon Is Far)* is an assemblage of wood, glass, and stone, over 9 feet tall and suggesting a form that should have been taller still. Wood slats have been arranged to grid the shape of an aerial balloon, which is rooted in stone blocks that could never get off the ground. It has fallen over, resting its weary, worried head on the earth, like Shelley's shattered statue of Ozymandias, the wreckage of a colossal statue of an ancient, forgotten king, who once ruled all he surveyed. But now, only the broken remnants of the statue can be found: "Nothing beside remains. Round the decay/Of that colossal wreck, boundless and bare/The lone and level sands stretch far away."

Visible within the wood balloon is an enormous glass globe—a clarified and gleaming idea that cannot be lofted into the air, that cannot escape the weight of its housing, that is going nowhere. Our most ambitious thoughts are earth-bound. They will not lift us to the skies.

But there are no final judgments in Averbuch's works, no lasting triumph of the tragic, of despair. Ultimately, there is an ambiguity of all hope and of all despair, of all sense of monumentality and commemoration, and of all cynicism and desperation. There is an intimate and intricate integration of hope and loss, of the victorious and the tragic. Each one portends the other.

For example, *The Dove Tower and Steps to the Bottom of a Pyramid* (2004), which is located at the University of Connecticut-Storrs, is an apt example of the inescapable connection between hope and the tragic. The work is in two parts: an inverted stone dove tower, standing on its top and at an angle, and a stone, stepped well, dropping into the lawn in front of the school's Information Technologies and Engineering building. It is a combination of opposing tensions and implications, a confrontation that reaches both to the depths and to the heavens. The visibly unstable, upside-down tower, in a work constructed only a few years after 9/11, is reminiscent of the destroyed towers of the World Trade Center, but the dove is a symbol of peace, as well as the bird that flew back to Noah with signs of emerging land, of deliverance. The inverted tower also refers to the columbaria that can be found throughout the Middle East. They are places

for collecting manure from birds to fertilize the land, and also places to bury the dead. The pyramid runs in the wrong direction, runs into the earth, but it is also taken from the stepped wells in India, in which one descends into the earth to obtain water, to locate the source of life. From the bottom of the sculpture's inverted pyramid, one cannot see the university, or the lawn, or the earth—but one can see the sky.

Similarly, *Divided World* (2000) finds an intricacy of tragedy and hope in one of the most politically charged, and politically tragic, places on earth. *Divided World* is located in Lavon, in the Galilee, in Israel—in the place of one of the most difficult and interminable conflicts of the modern world. The work is located on a hilltop, immediately above an area half of whose inhabitants are Arab and half are Jewish. It contains two stone stairways, built out of stones from destroyed houses in the area—the stones are dense with the tragic history of the place. The stairways are mirror images of each other, but running in opposite directions and running in parallel—they do not meet. Between them extend two arches, each one rising from one of the stairways, the two stretching towards each other—but they do not meet. Two boulders hang from chains, hang down from the ends of the arches, and the boulders do meet, but more like fists than like a clasping of hands.

The overall form of the work was inspired by the observatories at Jantar Mantar in India, but this is no image of reaching towards the stars. *Divided World* speaks of broken dreams and continually lost possibilities, and it also speaks of something else. As one changes one's perspective by walking around the sculpture, the stairways seem to join and the arches seem to blend into one. The movement that appears as one moves about the work is like the closing and separating of doors, but it is also like the fusion of the parts into a single conception, into a joining together of oppositions. And when one looks closely at the two boulders, one sees that the point of contact is slight, and delicate, barely there. For all their hard mass, they touch gently, like the brushing of a hand across a cheek, like a breath gliding along the hairs of the skin—like a kiss.

*Avanim Vetseadim (Steps and Stones)* (2008), at Gezer Park, in Leawood, Kansas, is a stone ladder reaching for the sky. But it is positioned in a pond, so that it is reflected in the water, it also stretches downward. An aspiration that reverses itself, and yet, in either direction, it presses towards the unreachable, towards the sky, or towards the immaterial reflection. And the horizon line is evaporated, the ground is dispelled, and as in the many works in which Averbuch suspends the horizon line above the ground, the point of gravity, of the dragging to the earth, is erased. The integration of earth and sky, the duplication of each in the other, is the artistic integration of transport beyond the degrading materiality with the quotidian world, with the weight of mortality. In the ambiguity of its reaching, *Avanim Vetseadim* configures an aspiration for something beyond the material, beyond the merely visible, that also stretches into the earthly, the tragic.

This is the complexity of hope, and despair: in the real world, each one is to be found in and behind the other. And this is the heart of Ilan Averbuch's contribution to public sculpture, his revised paradigm for public sculpture. His sense of hope that is always qualified but never eradicated by despair and loss is a matured judgment, a judgment taught by life experience. It stands in place of the exhortations of simplified, uncomplicated, cartoon-like virtues that are the mark of traditional public works, of the unqualified commemorations of standard memorials that express our admiration but not our sense of reality. Averbuch's is the art of the tempered judgment of the mature mind, of the mind that faces the truths of life. In that, he achieves one of the highest accomplishments of art: to mature the minds of the society in which it occurs. And the maturing of the mind is both a renewed possibility of hope and a recognition of the inevitability of the tragic.

* Mark Daniel Cohen is a writer and public speaker on philosophy, contemporary art, and aesthetics with over 400 book chapters, articles, art reviews, and essays in publication in a variety of art exhibition catalogues and commercial, academic, and art school journals. He is the Editor of *Hyperion: On the Future of Aesthetics*, an e-journal published by The Nietzsche Circle, a philosophical society based in New York City (http://www.nietzschecircle.com/hyperion.html), and he is the Assistant Dean of the European Graduate School (EGS), Saas-Fee, Switzerland.

WORKS

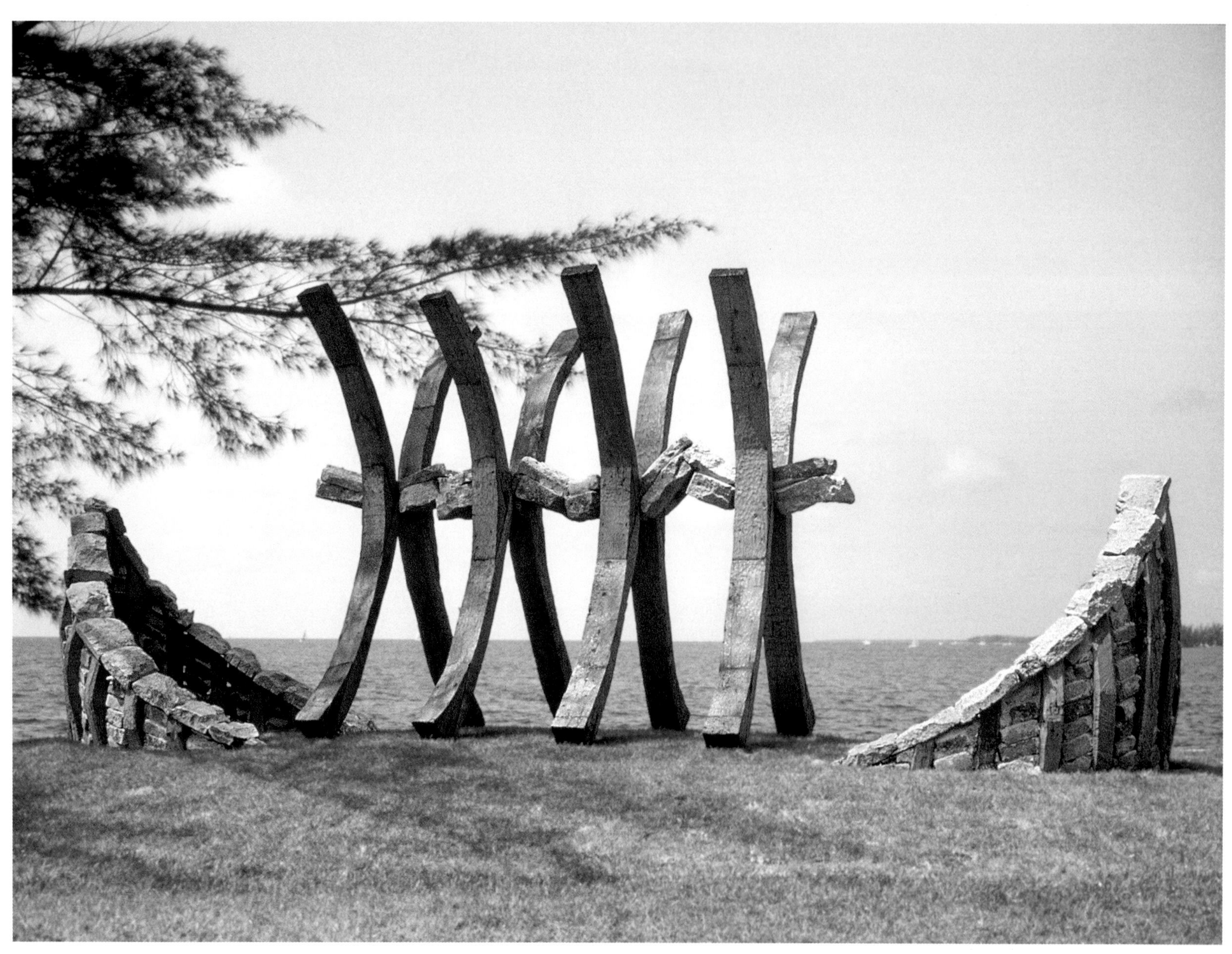

**Journey's End**, 1985
Wood, stone, steel
12 x 30 x 8 feet
Collection of Florida International University,
Miami, Florida

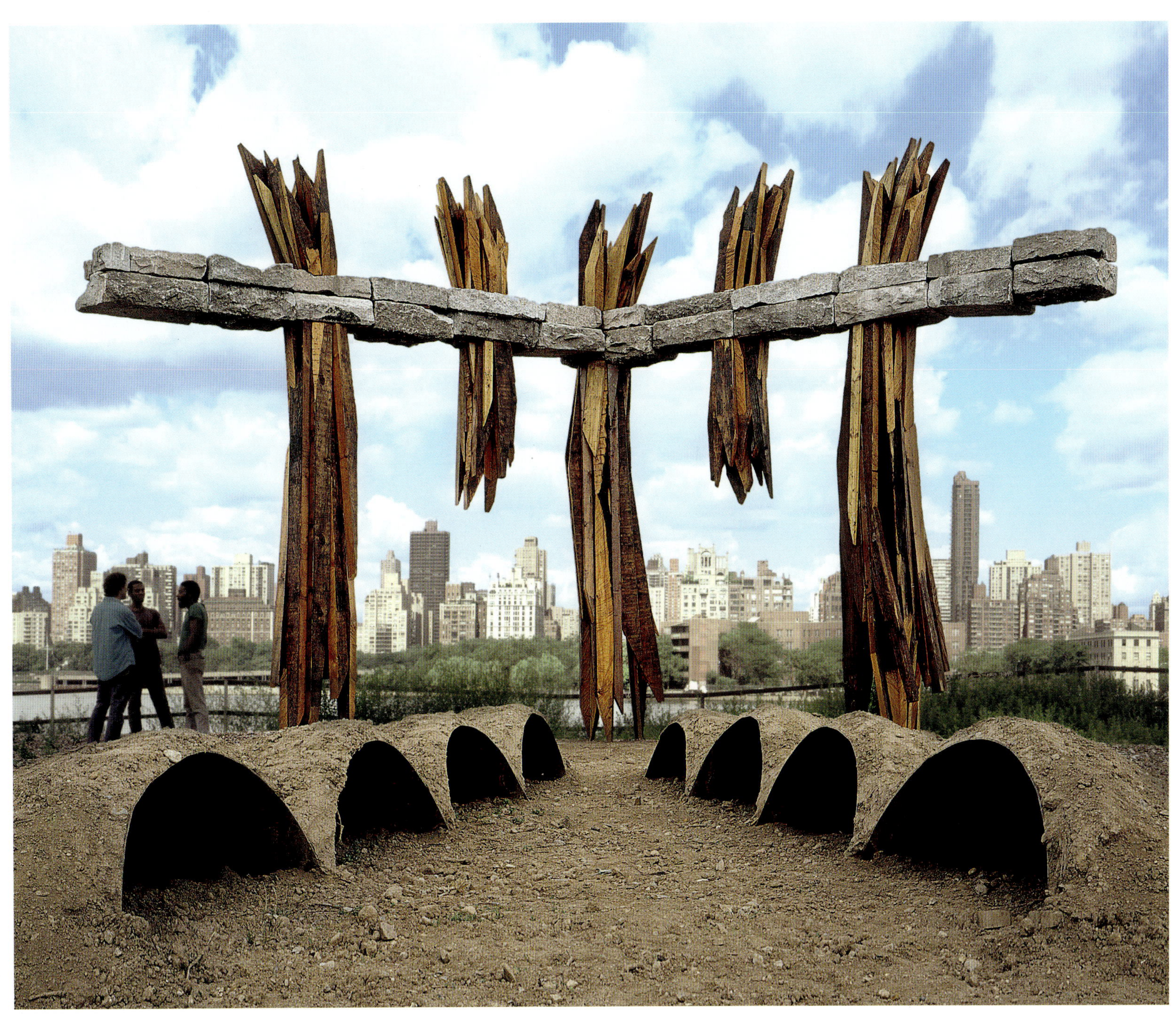

**Songs of Love and Hate**, 1989
Wood, stone, earth
15 x 35 x 30 feet
Pictured at Socrates Sculpture Park, New York, New York
Private Collection, California

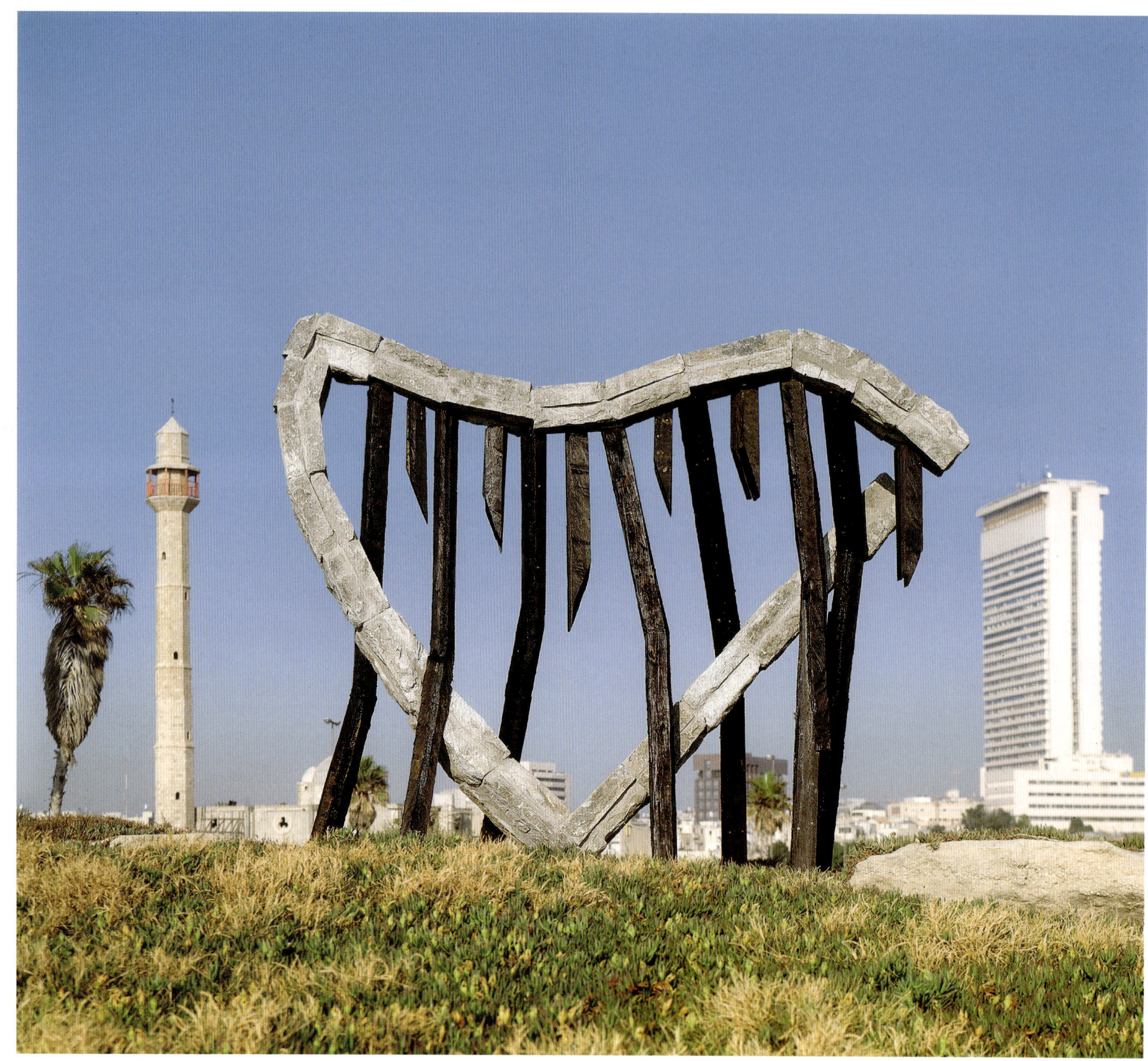

**Harp the Sea and the Quiet Wind**, 1989
Wood, stone, steel
15 x 21 x 8 feet
Tel Aviv-Jaffa, Israel
Collection of the Tel Aviv Museum of Art,
Tel Aviv, Israel

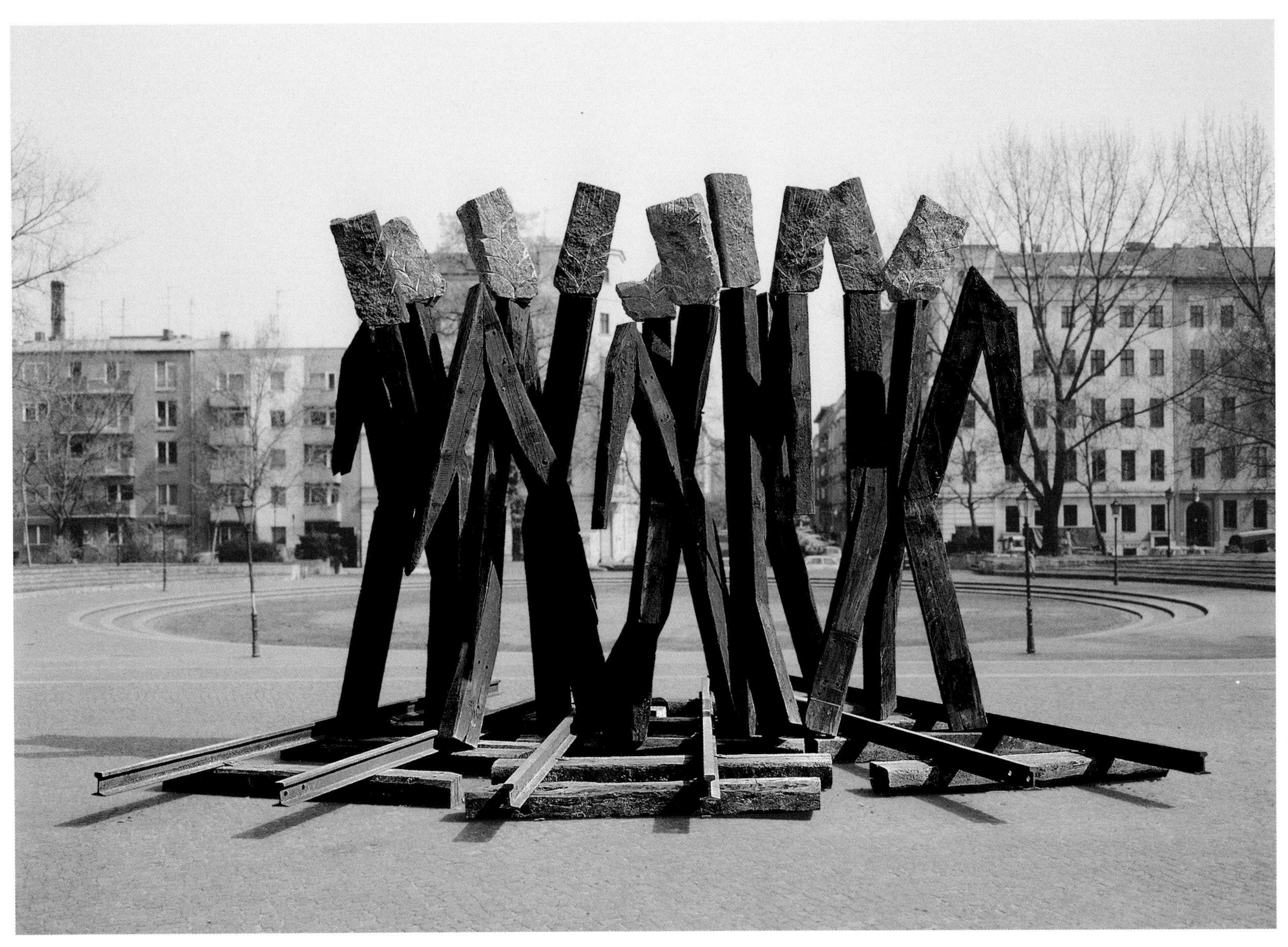

**Wheat in Berlin**, 1987
Wood, stone, steel
11 1/2 x 14 1/2 x 14 1/2 feet
Pictured at Marianenplatz, Berlin
The Open Muesum, Omer, Israel

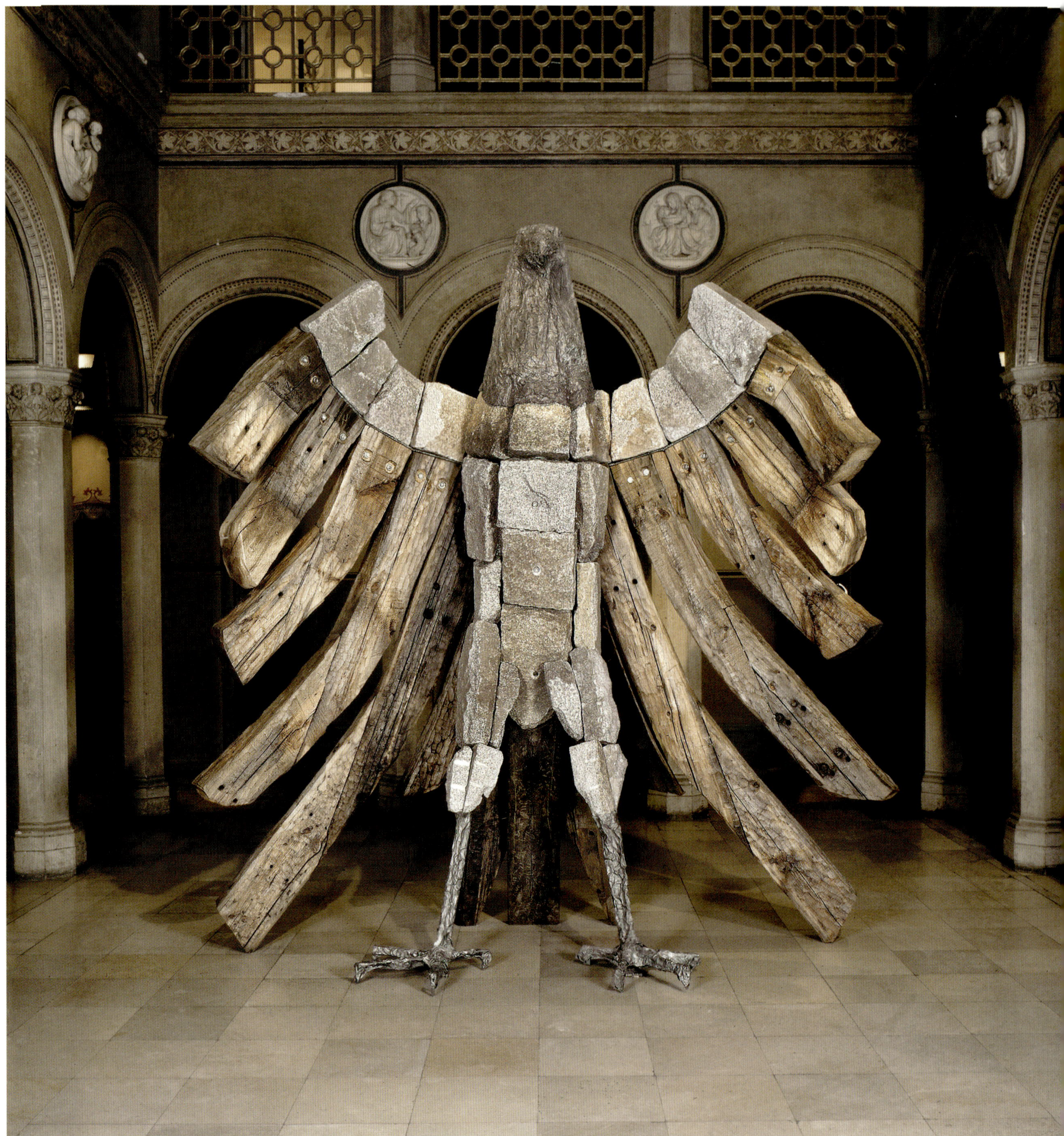

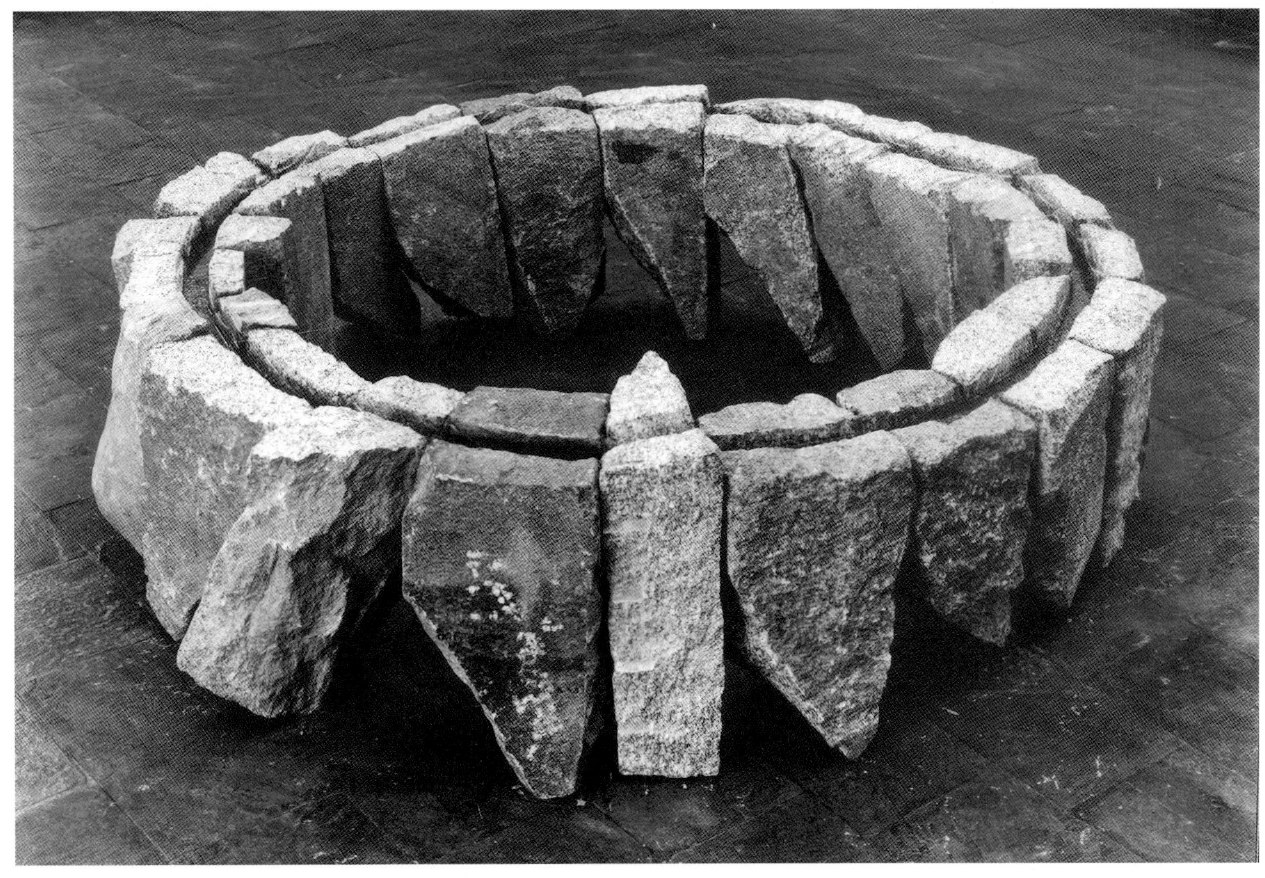

**Inherited Memories**, 1985
Stone, wood, lead
9 x 10 x 3 feet
Pictured at Künstlerhaus Bethanien, Berlin
Private Collection, Canada

**Meeting**, 1985
Stone, water
20 x 78 x 78 inches
Hamburg Peace Biennale
Lutz Teutloff Collection, Bielefeld,
Germany

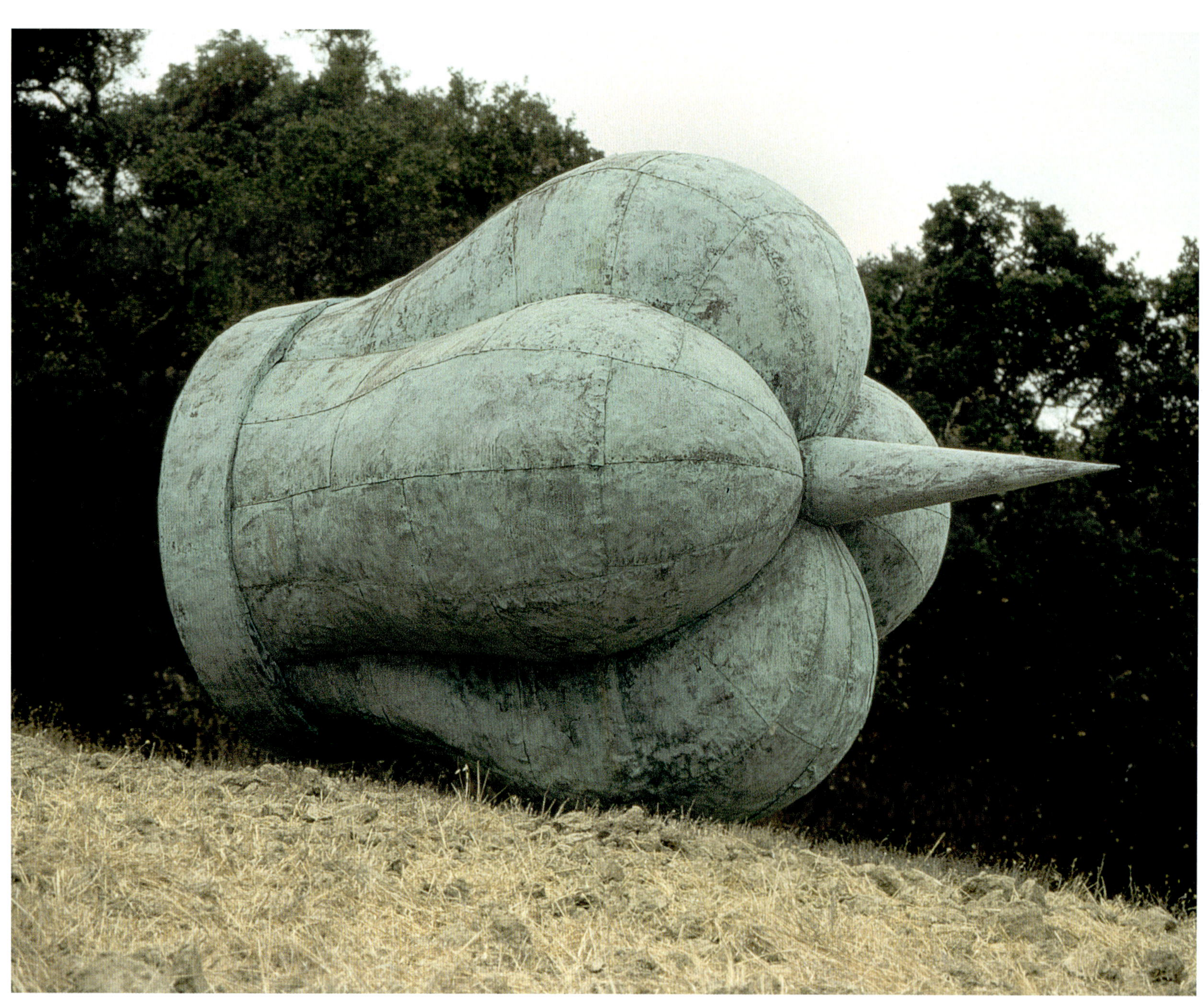

**After the Reign**, 1990
Wood, copper
10 x 15 x 10 feet
Runnymede Sculpture Farm,
Woodside, California

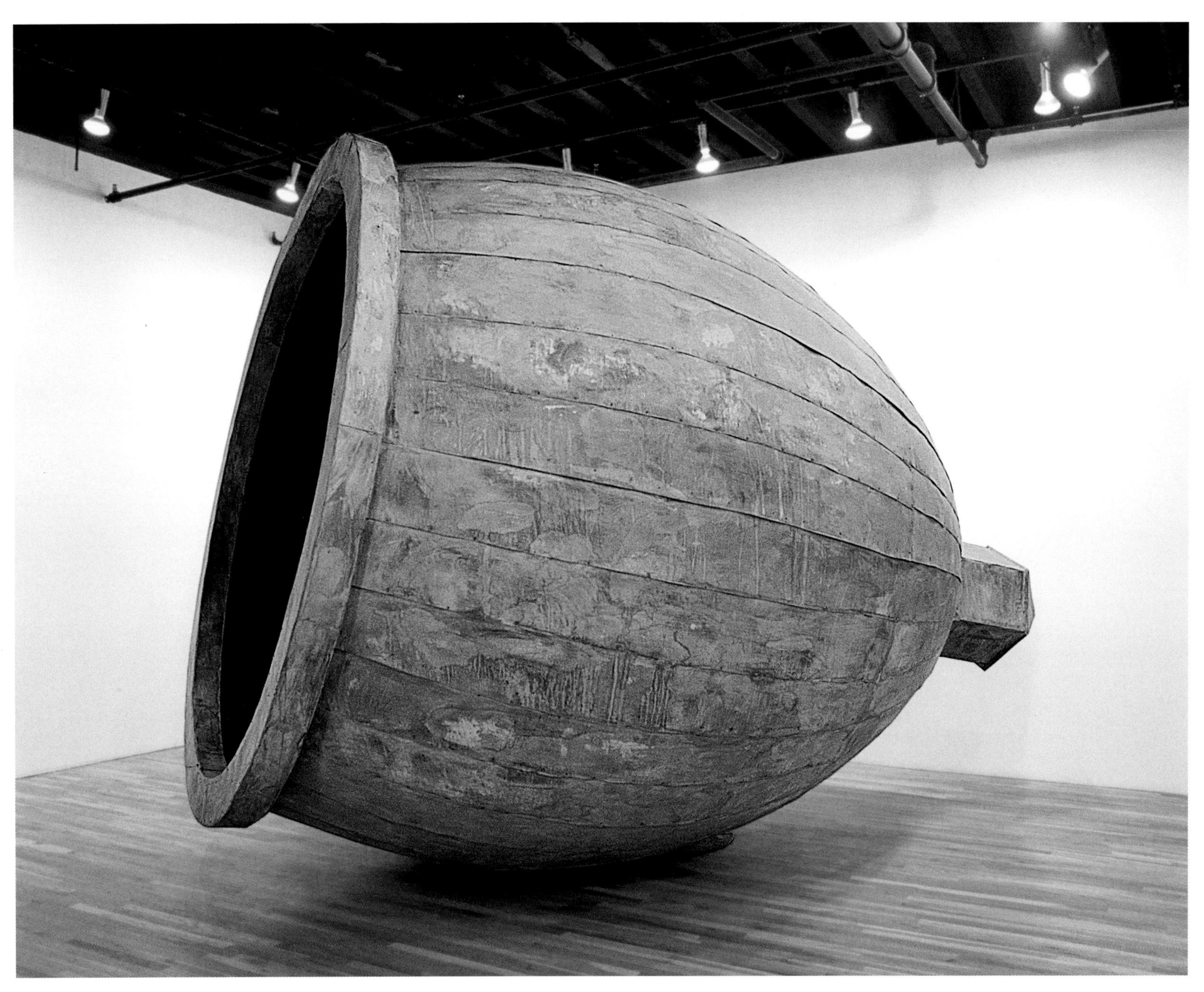

**The Fall**, 1989
Wood, copper
10 1/2 x 15 1/2 x 10 feet
Runnymede Sculpture Farm, Woodside,
California

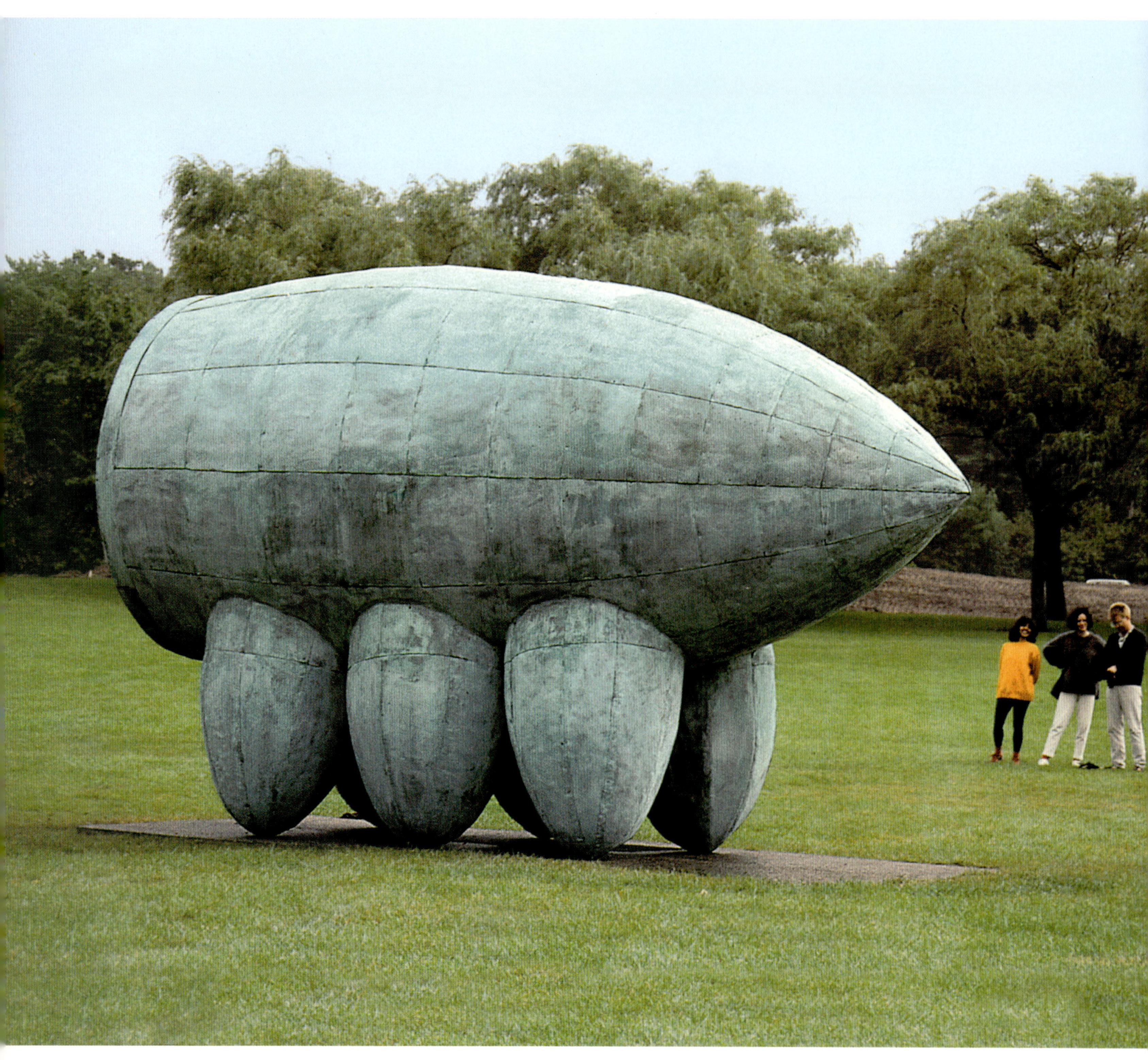

**She Wolf**, 1995
Copper, wood
14 x 20 x 9 feet
Brock University, St. Catharines, Canada
Lutz Teutloff Collection, Bielefeld, Germany

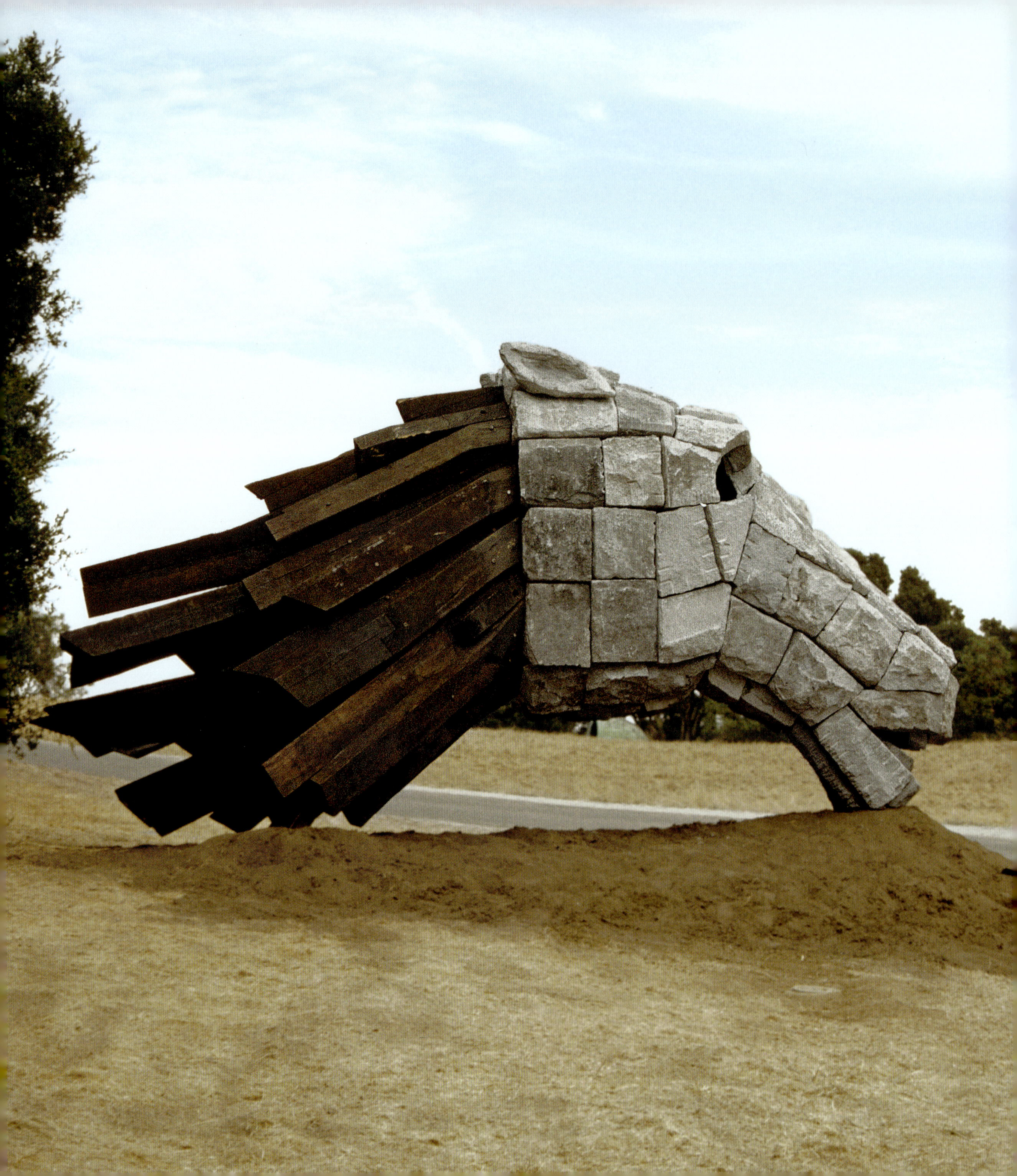

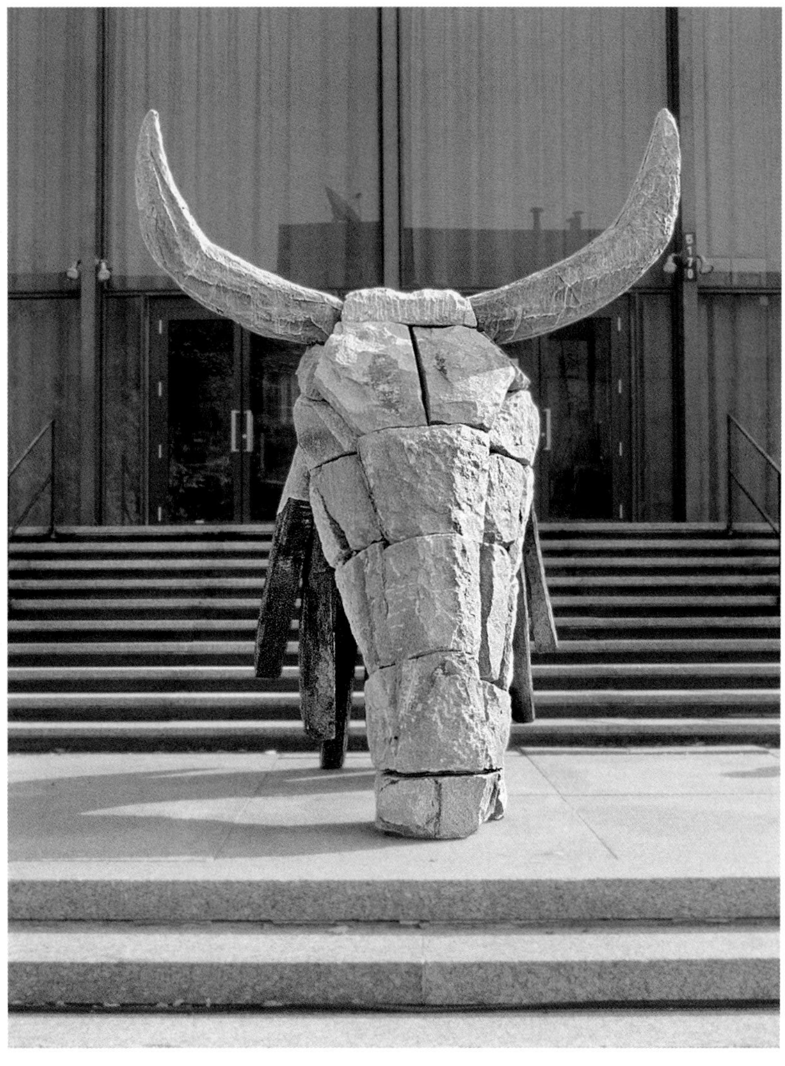

**Horse's Head**, 1993
Stone, wood
11 x 28 x 8 feet
Runnymede Sculpture Farm,
Woodside, California

**Sacrifice**, 1987
Wood, stone, lead
10 x 8 x 8 feet
Saidye Bronfman Center for the Arts,
Montreal, Canada

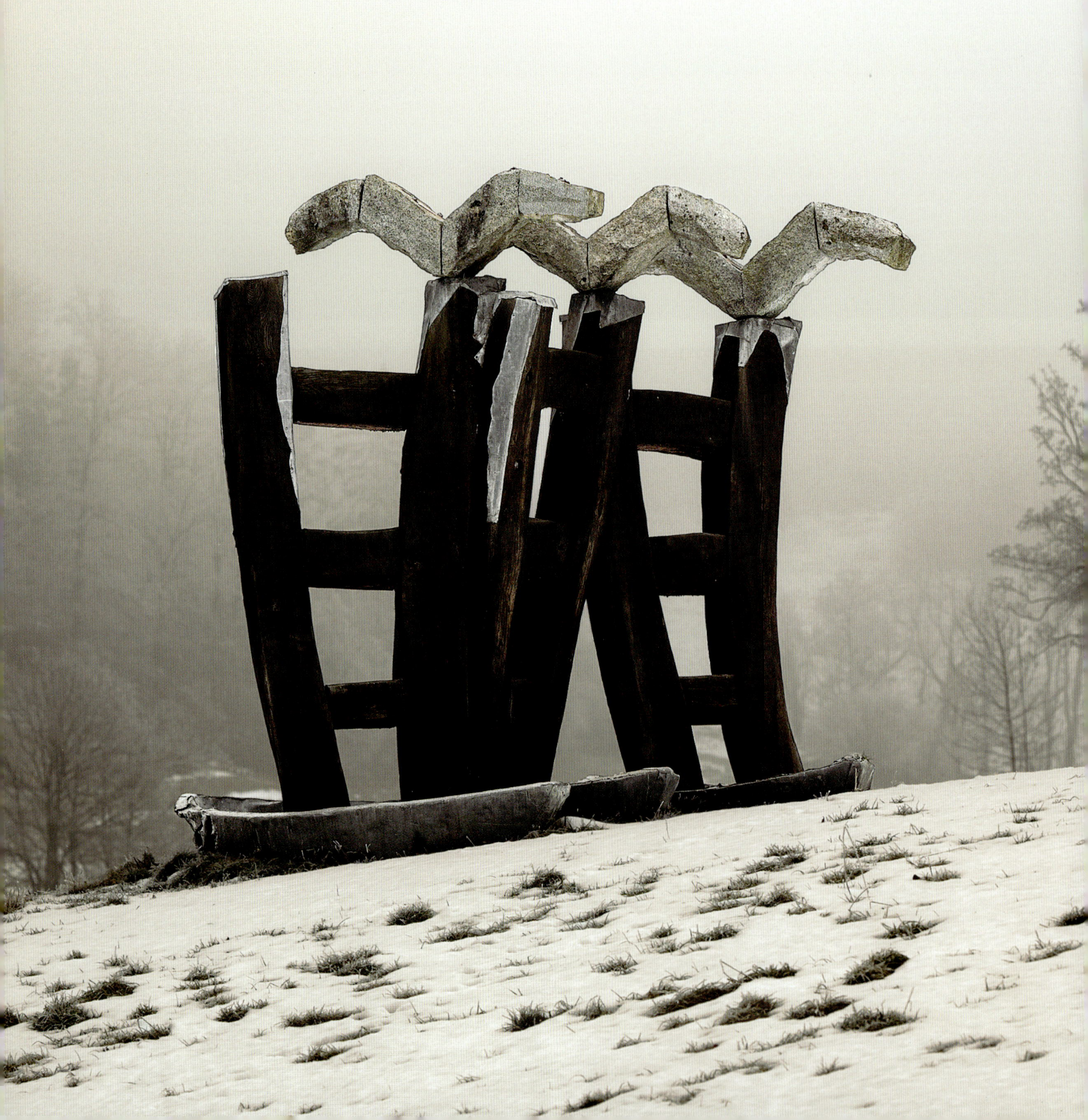

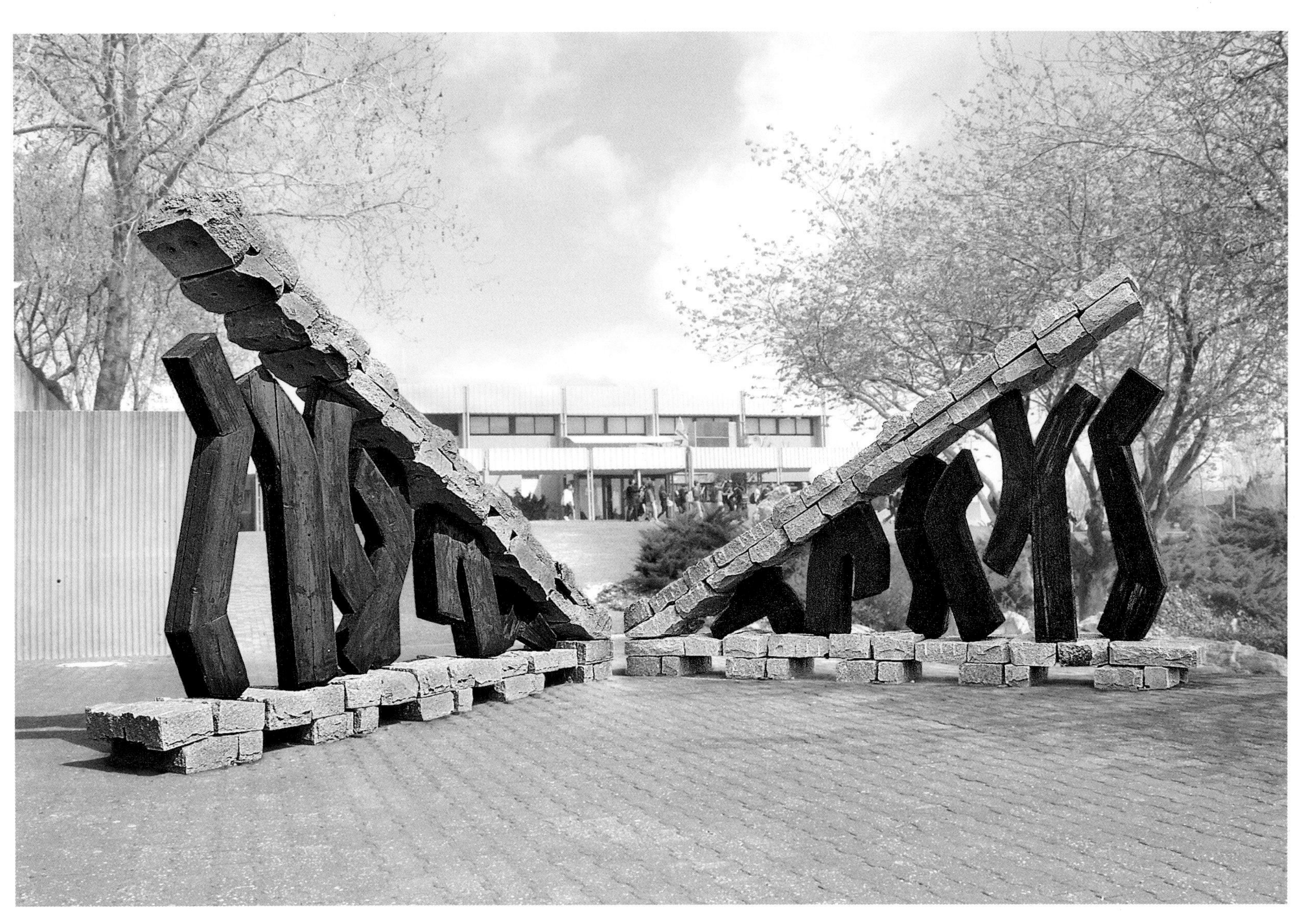

**Silent Seas**, 1992
Wood, stone, lead
10 x 12 x 10 feet
Schoenthal Monastery, Switzerland

**Deus Ex Machina**, 1991
Wood, Stone
10 x 26 x 16 feet
The Open Museum, Tefen, Israel

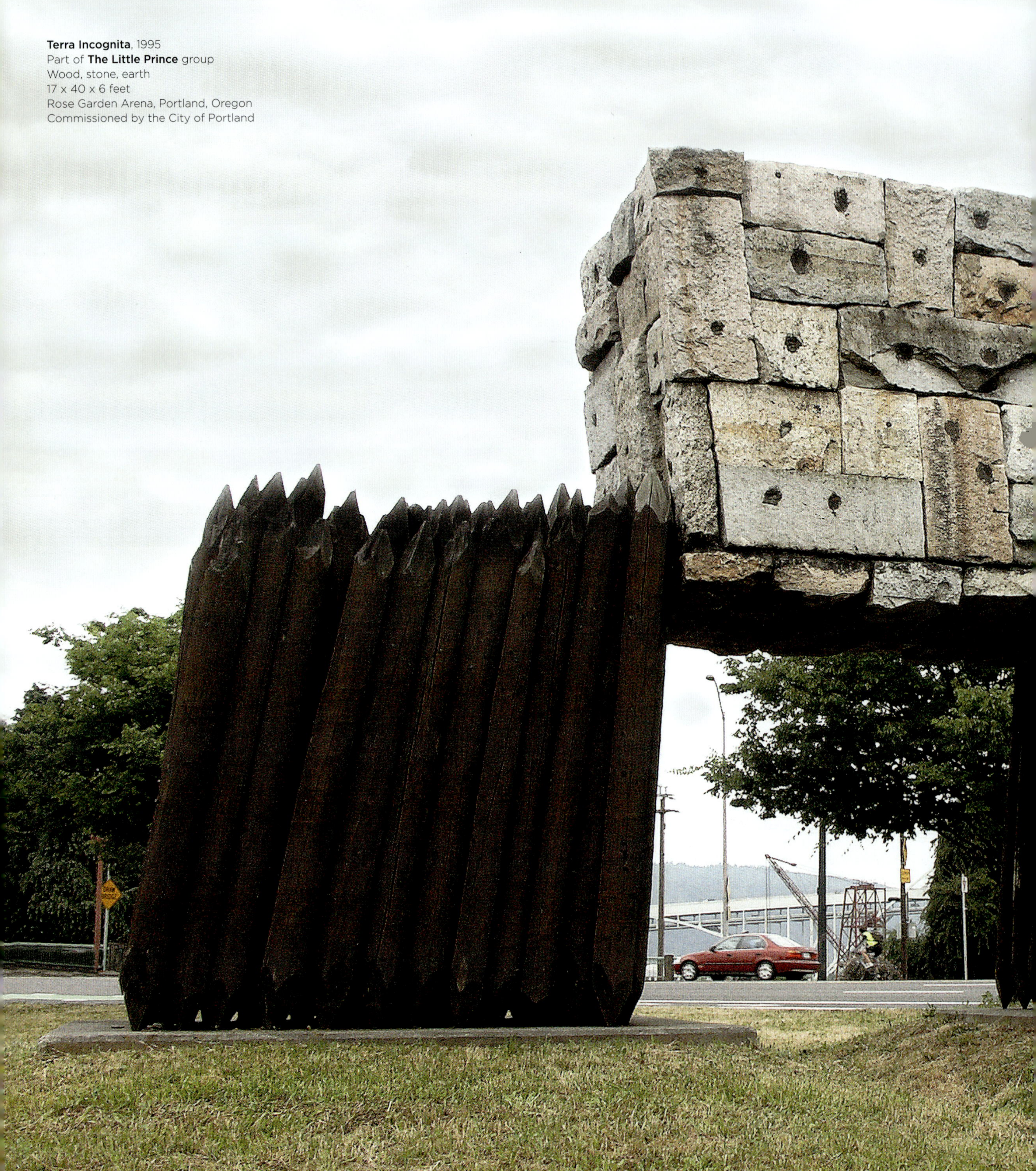

**Terra Incognita**, 1995
Part of **The Little Prince** group
Wood, stone, earth
17 x 40 x 6 feet
Rose Garden Arena, Portland, Oregon
Commissioned by the City of Portland

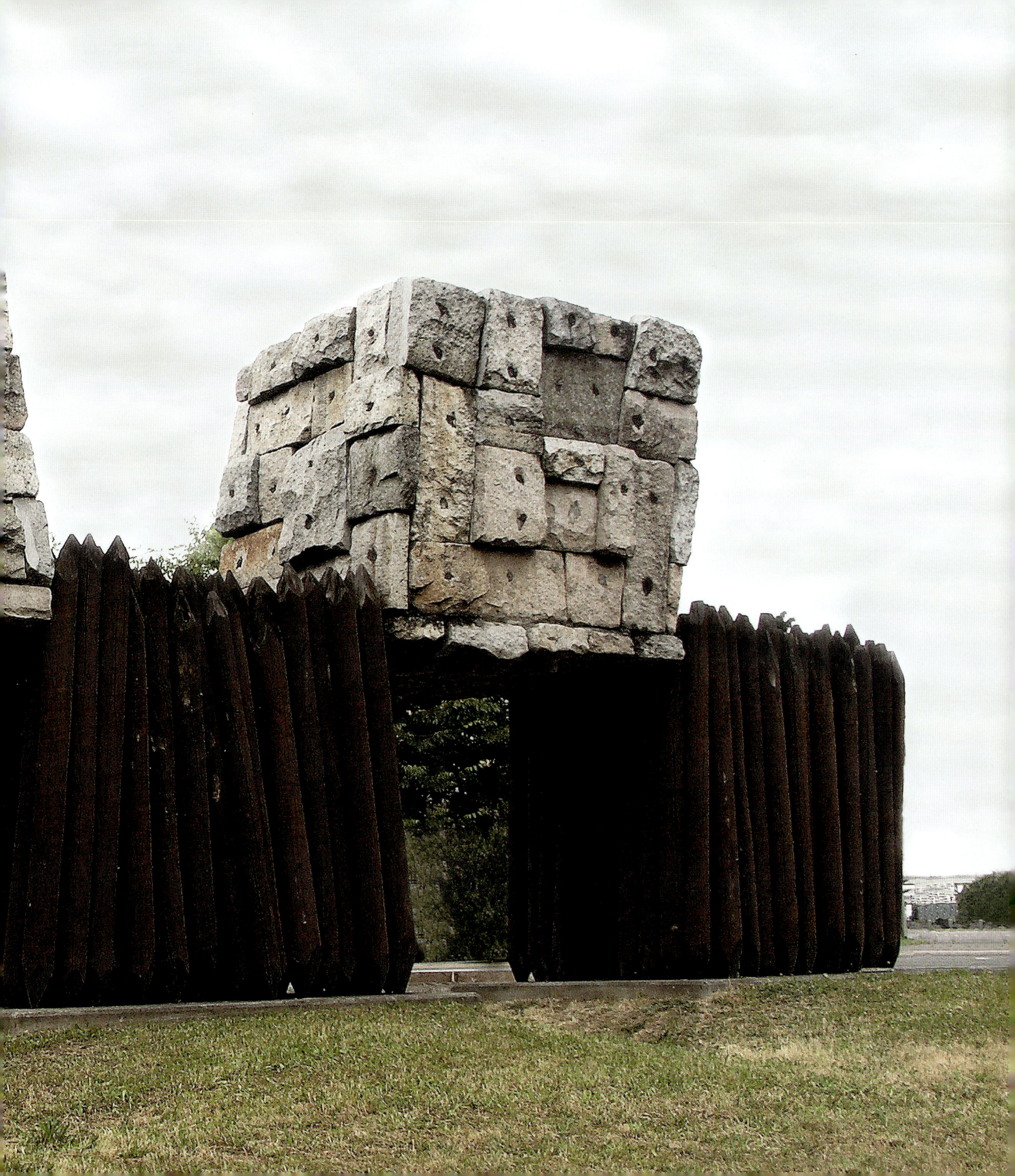

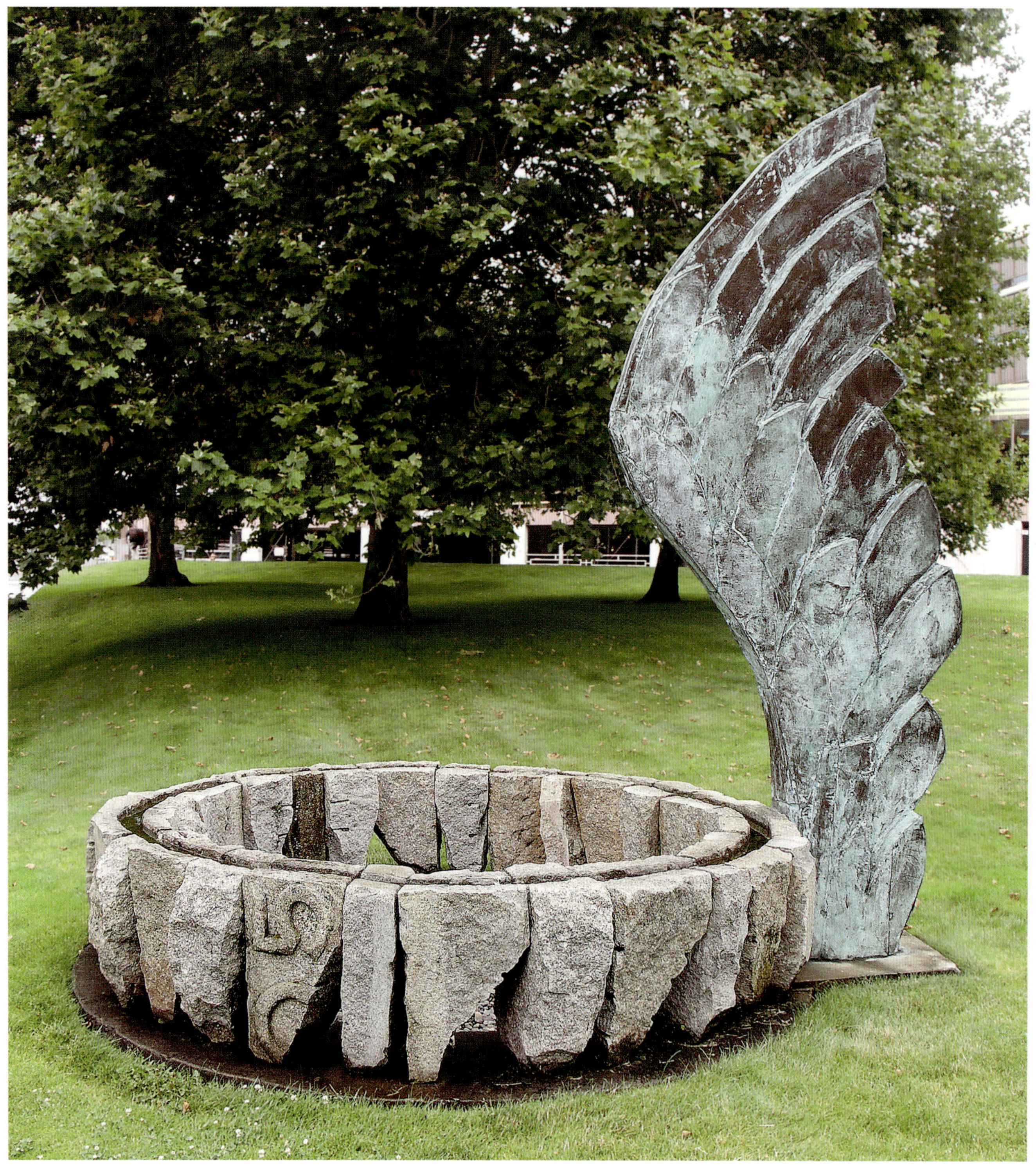

**Stone, Water, and Heaven**, 1995
Part of **The Little Prince** group
Stone, copper, water
10 x 10 x 9 feet
Rose Garden Arena, Portland, Oregon
Commissioned by the City of Portland

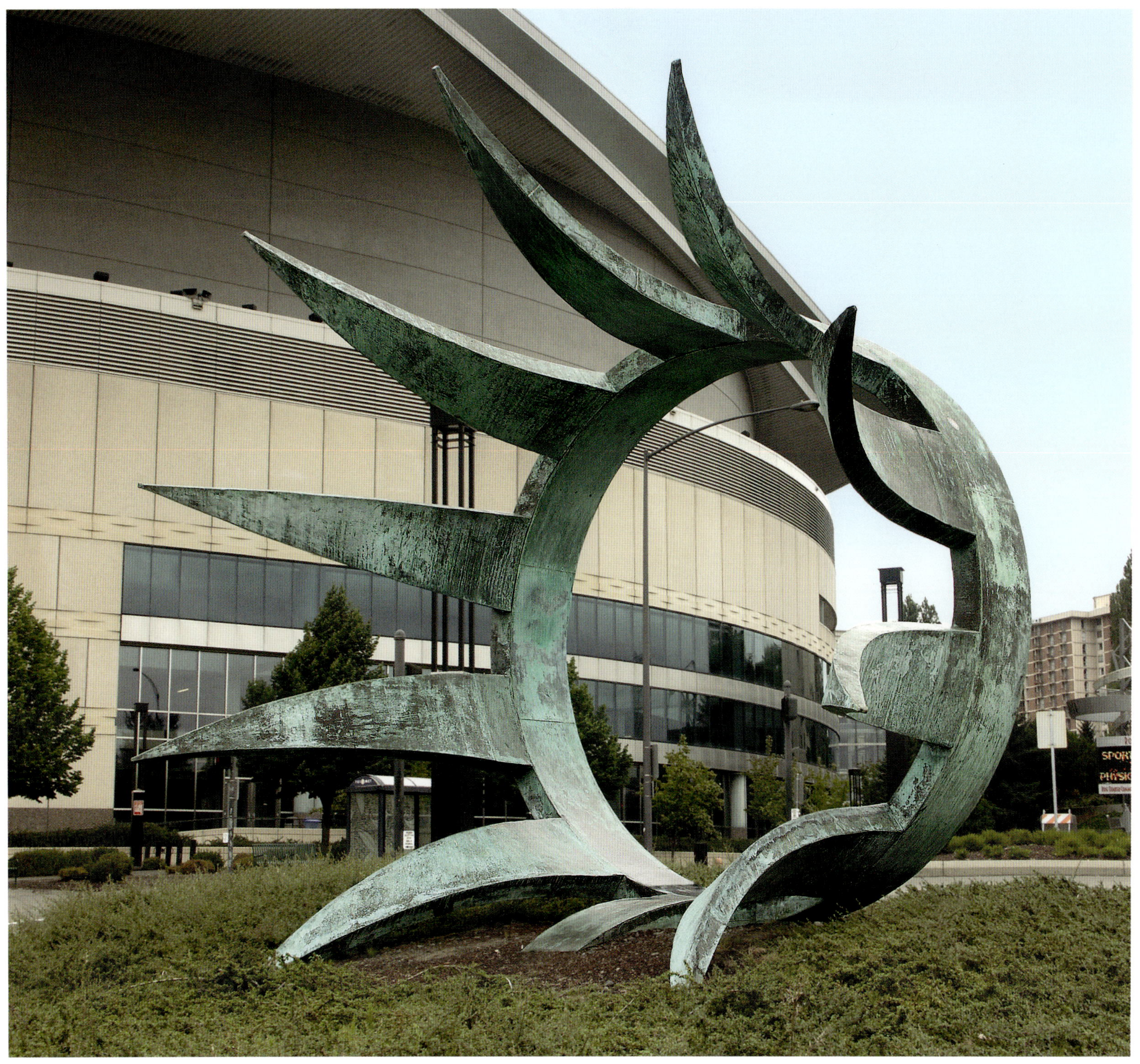

**The Little Prince**, 1995
Part of **The Little Prince** group
Copper
16 x 12 x 11 feet
Rose Garden Arena, Portland, Oregon
Commissioned by the City of Portland

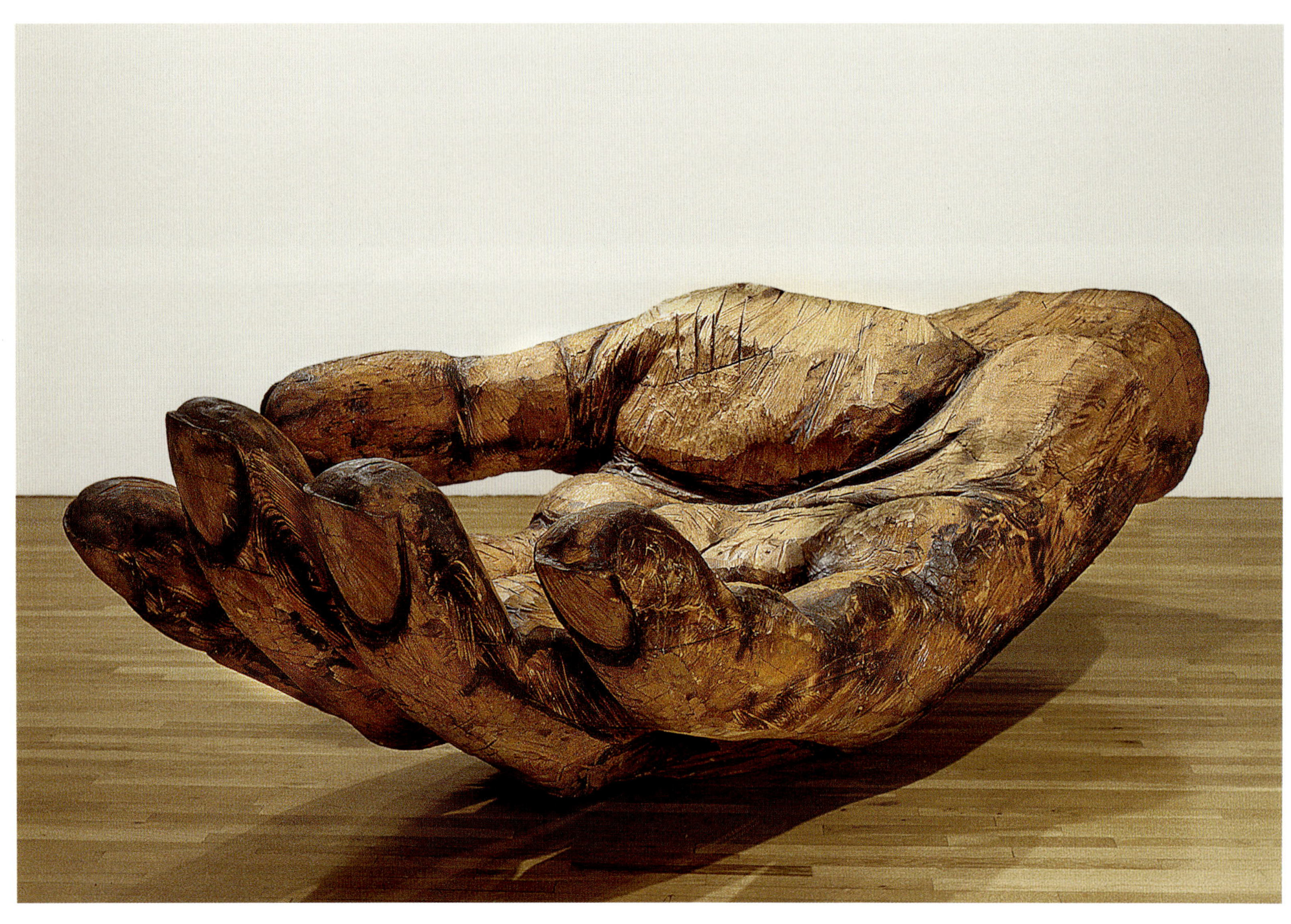

**Lost at Sea**, 1999
Wood
3 x 10 x 6 feet
Private Collection, California

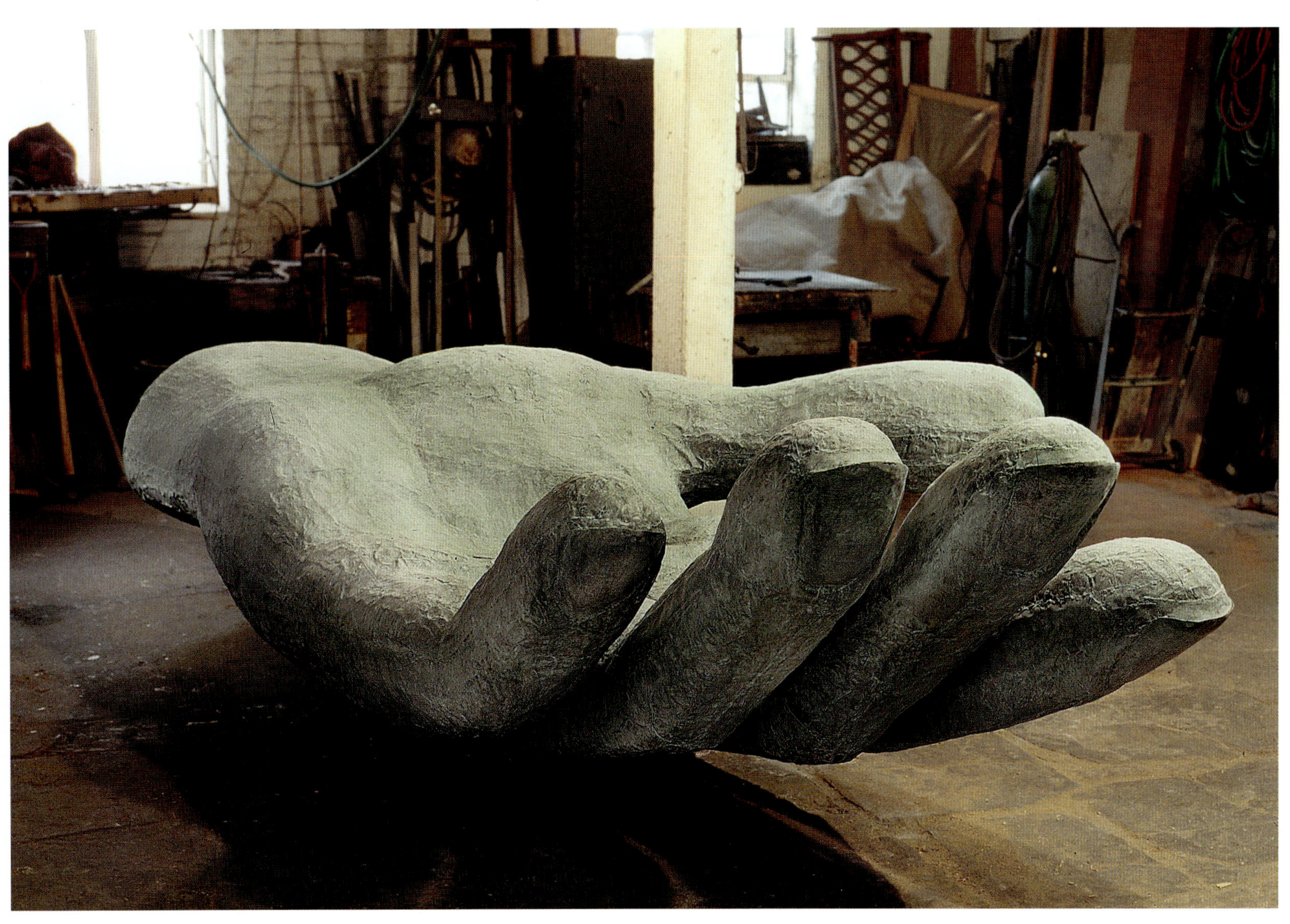

**Sky Is My Mirror**, 1999
Copper
42 x 140 x 84 inches
Lutz Teutloff Collection, Bielefeld, Germany

**In the End of Utopia (The Big Balloon Is Far)**, 1999
Wood, glass, stone
9 x 13 x 7 1/2 feet
Shown at the Katonah Museum of Art, Katonah, New York

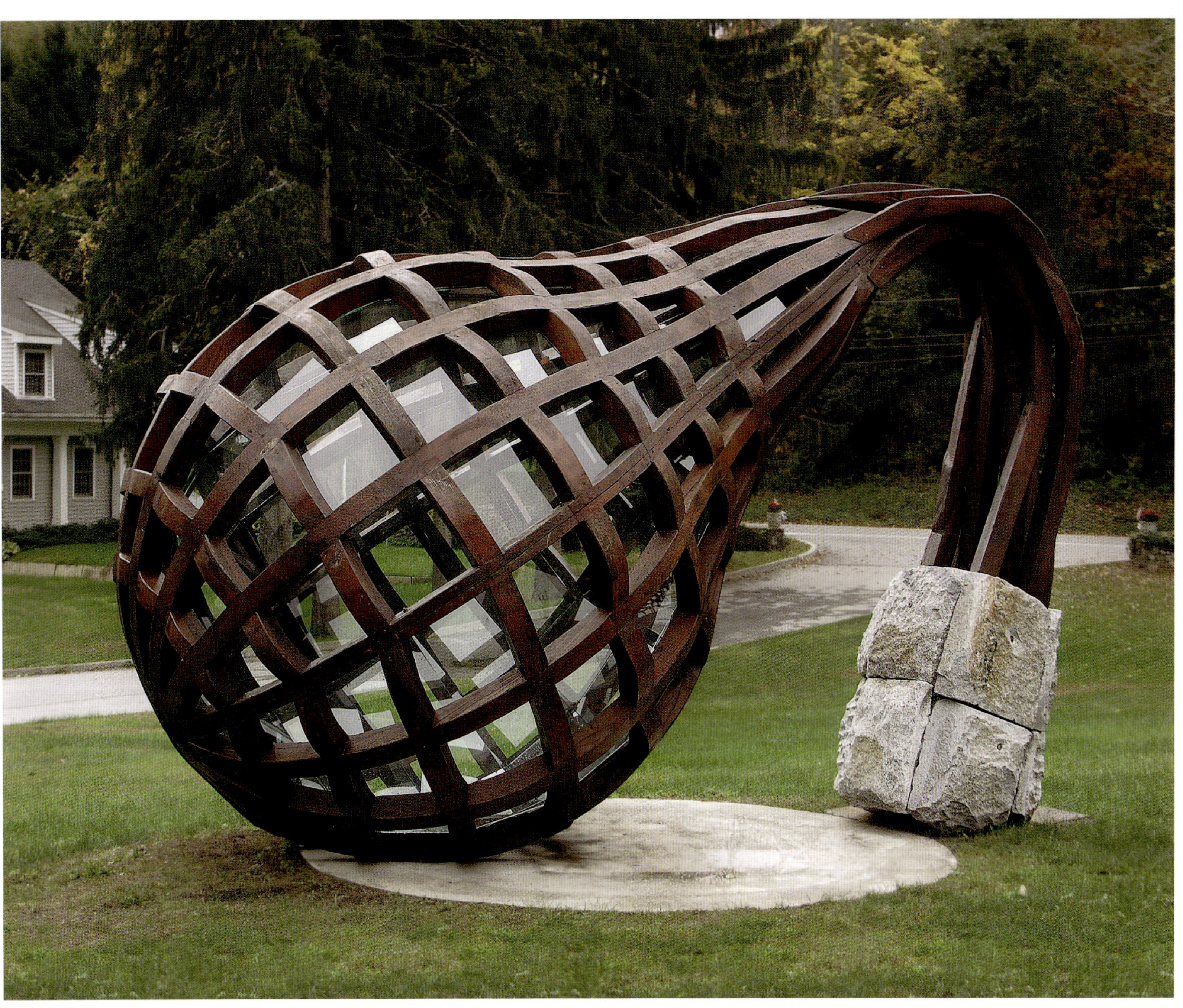

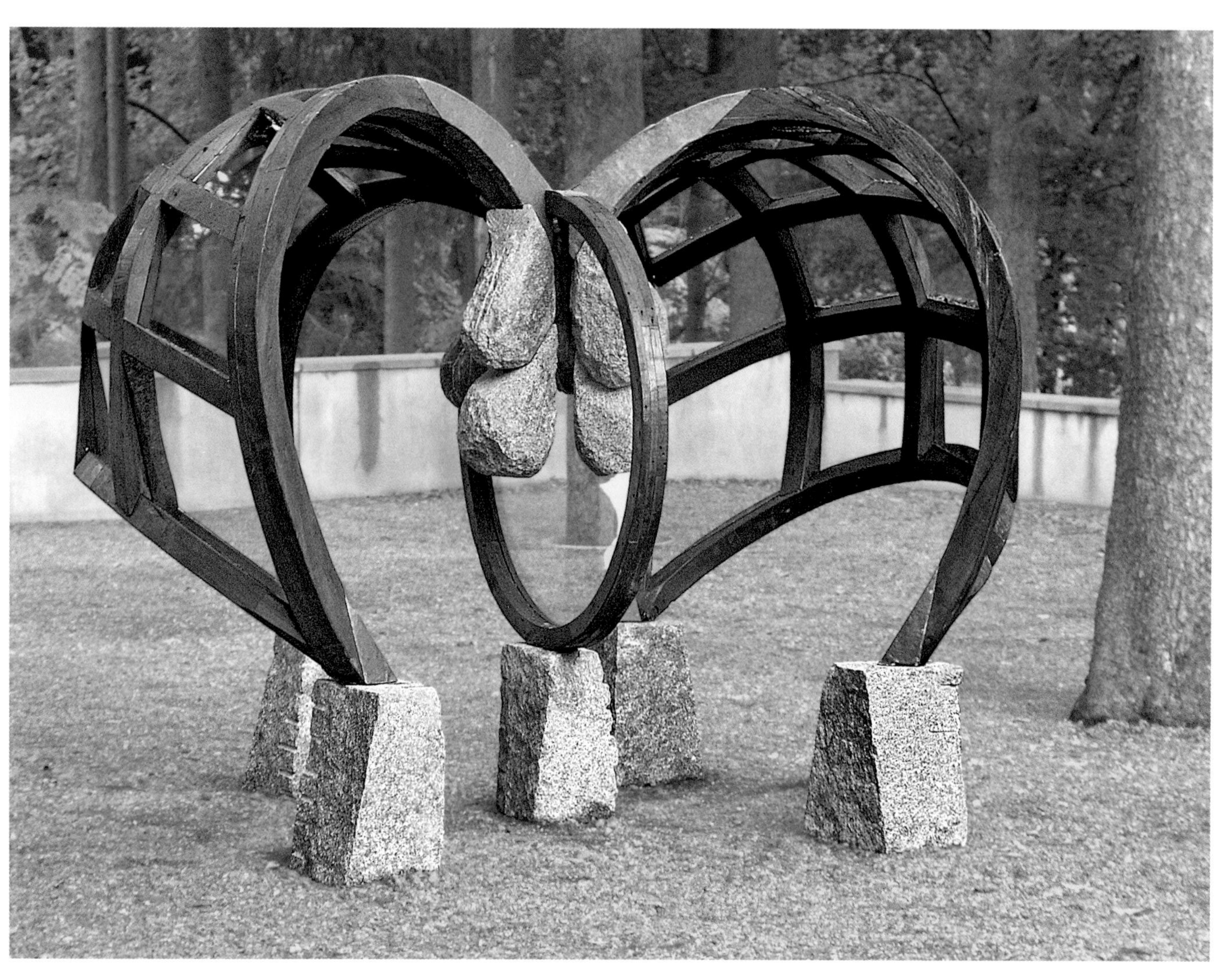

**Narcissus and the Desire to Fly**, 1999
Lead, wood, glass, stone
94 x 127 x 77 inches

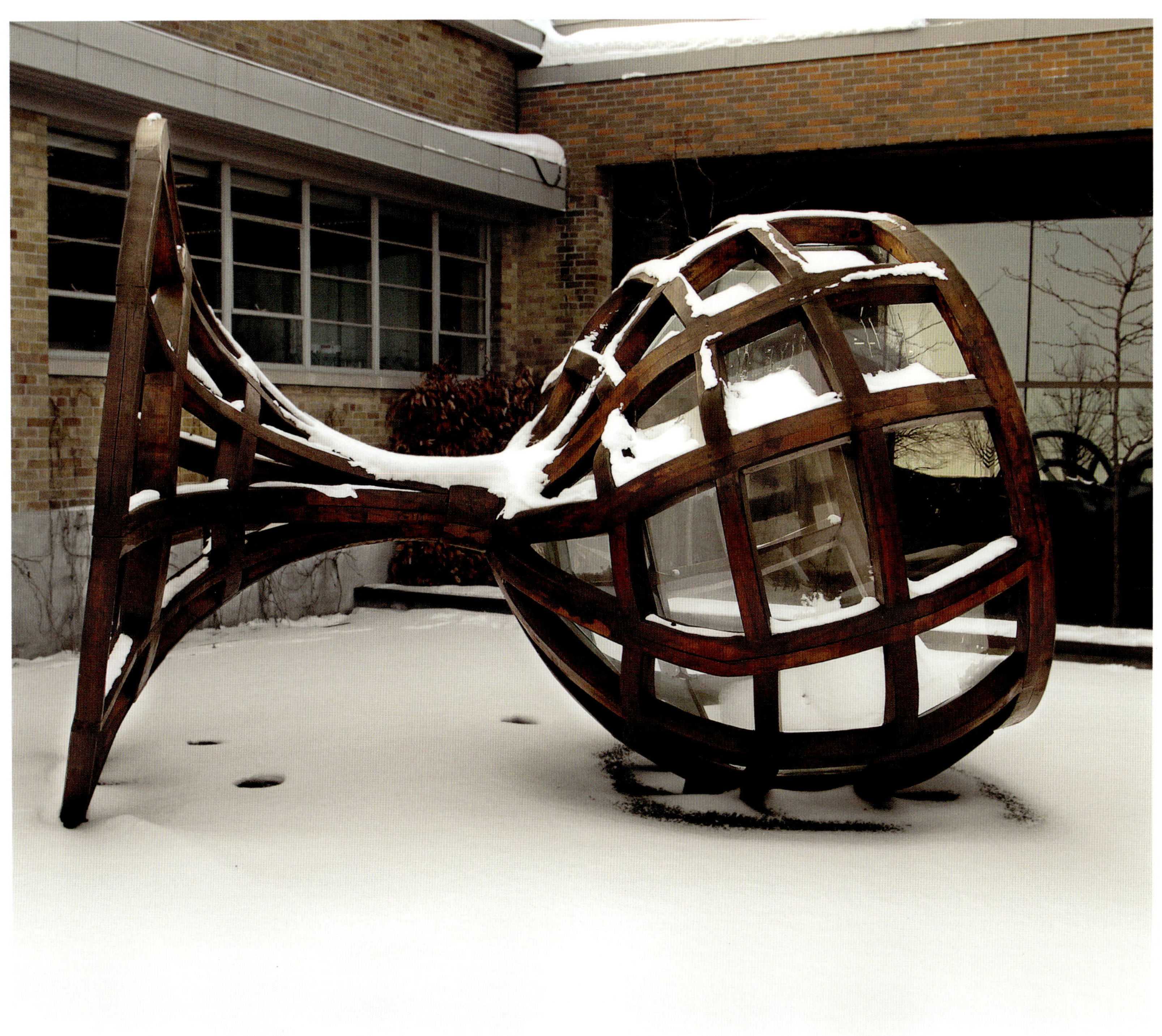

**Time Passing**, 1997
Wood, glass
10 x 15 x 16 feet
A1 Label Corporation, Toronto, Canada

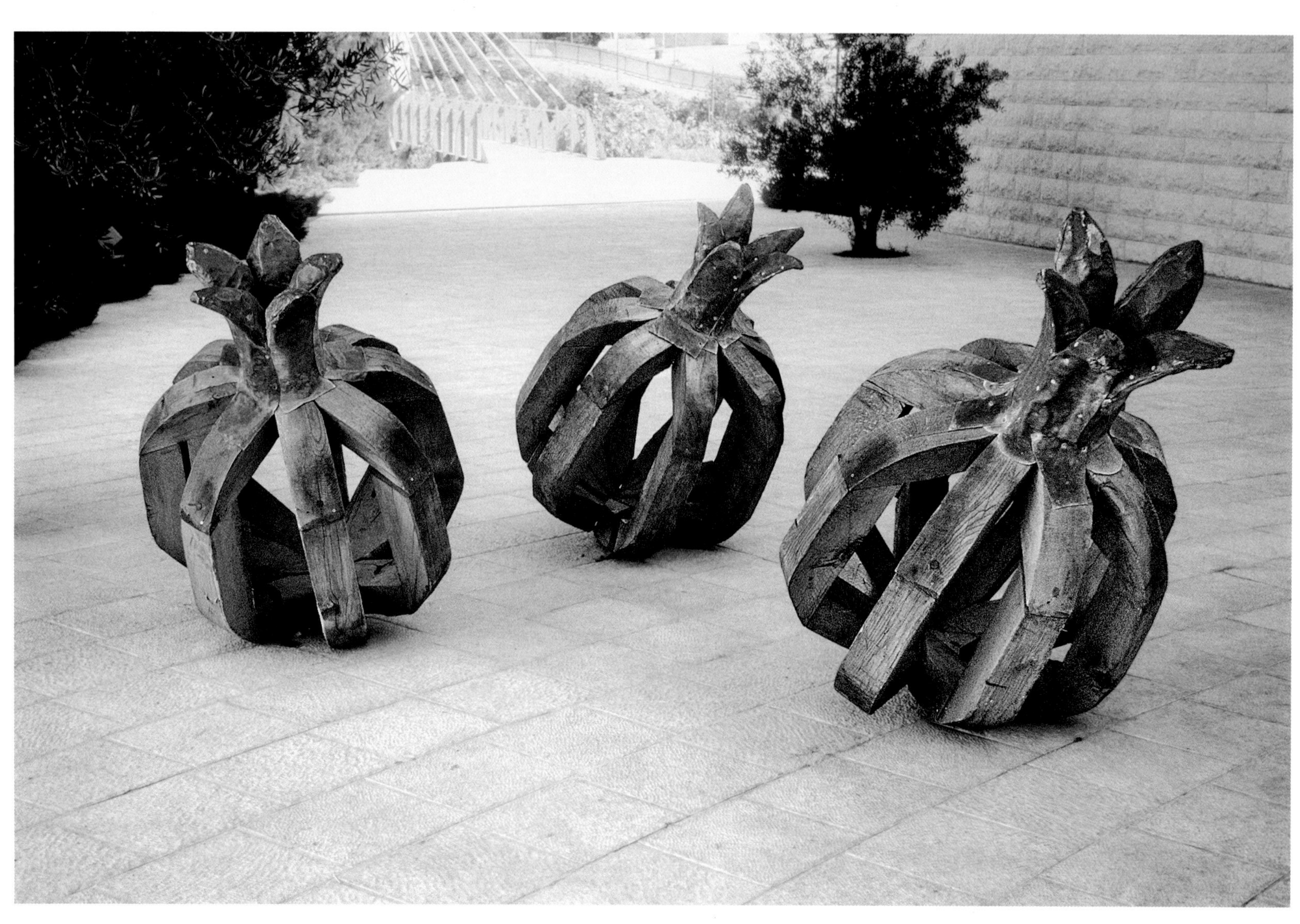

**Rib Grenade (Pomegranate)**, 1991
Wood, lead
66 x 108 x 48 inches
Supreme Court Building, Jerusalem, Israel
Collection of the Israel Museum of Art, Jerusalem, Israel

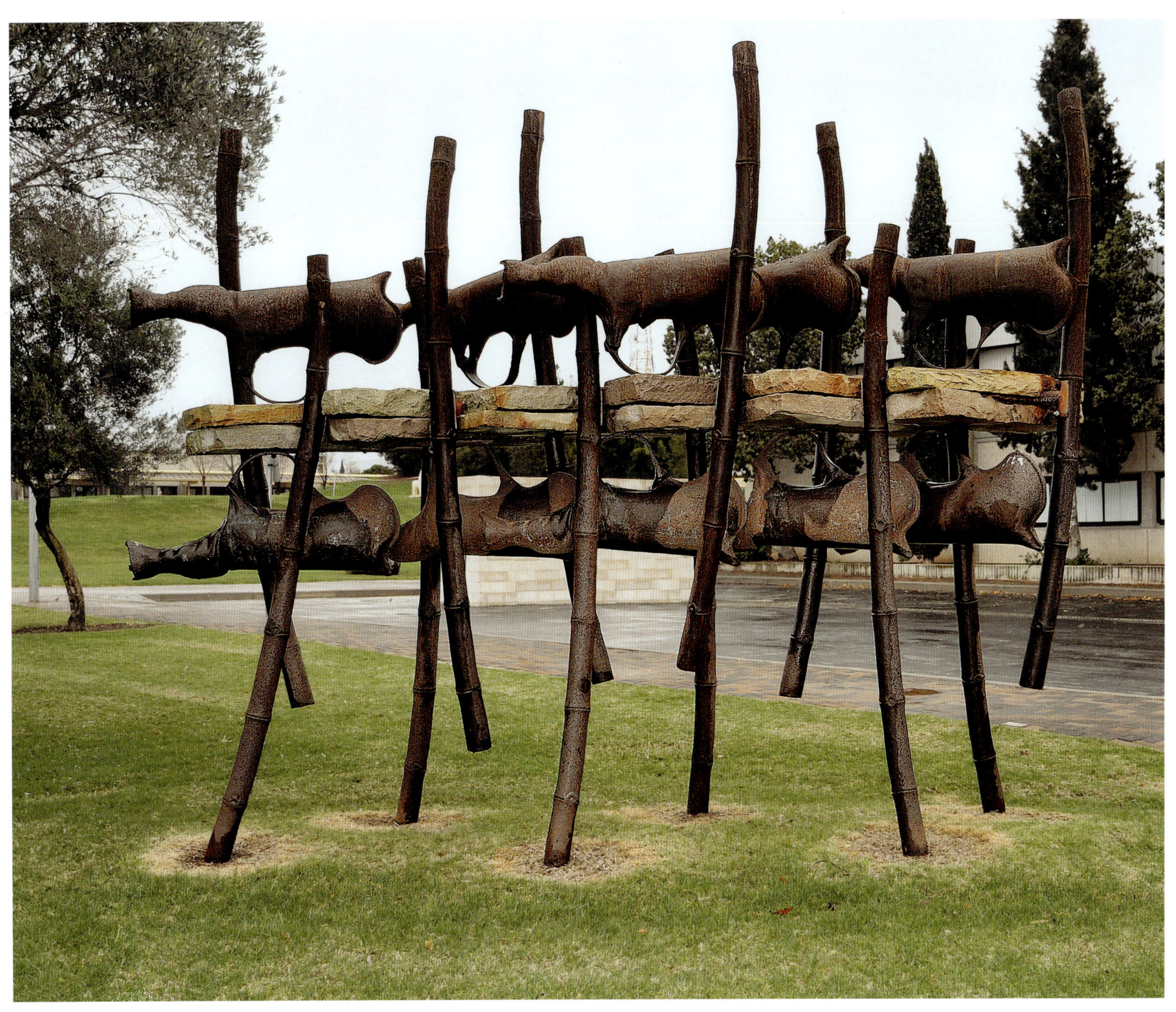

**The River**, 1996
Cast iron, stone
10 x 13 x 3 1/2 feet
The Open Museum, Tefen, Israel

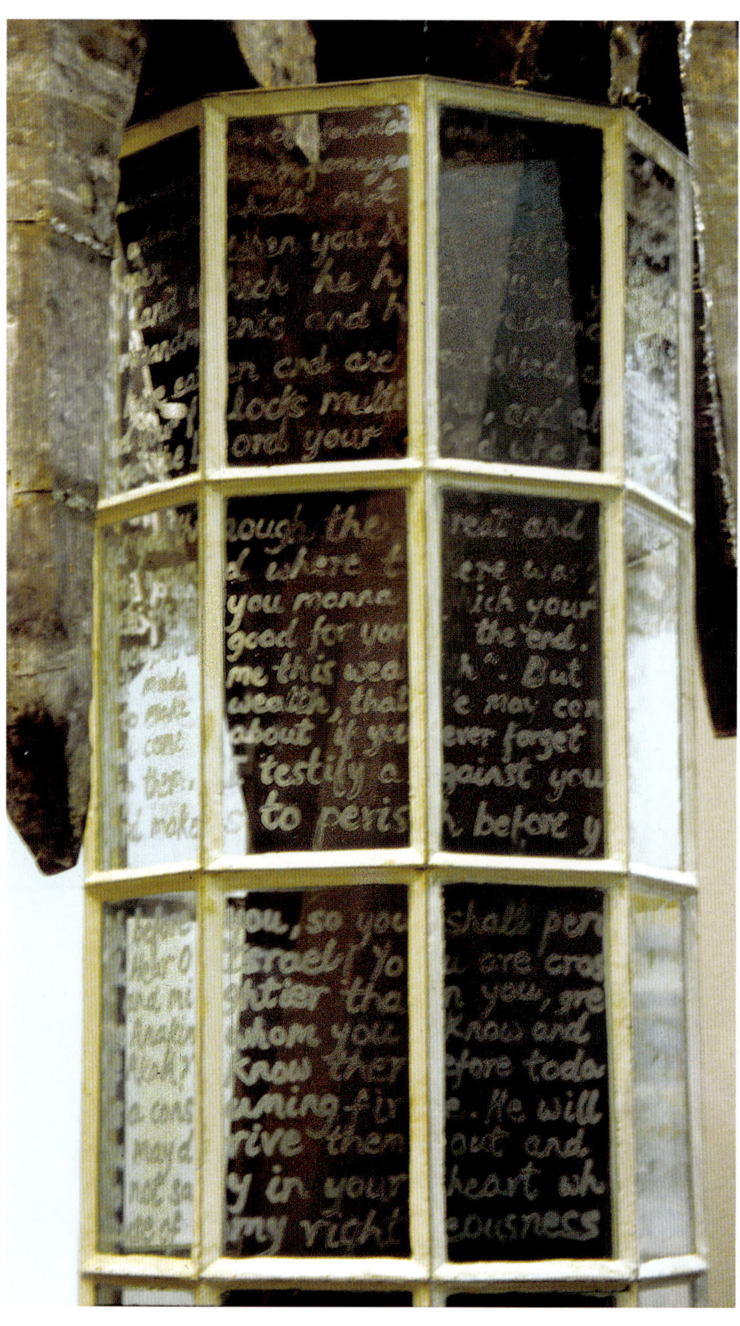

**The Forest**, 1999
Steel, glass, wood, stone, lead
13 x 27 x 27 feet
Shown at the Katonah Museum of Art, Katonah, New York

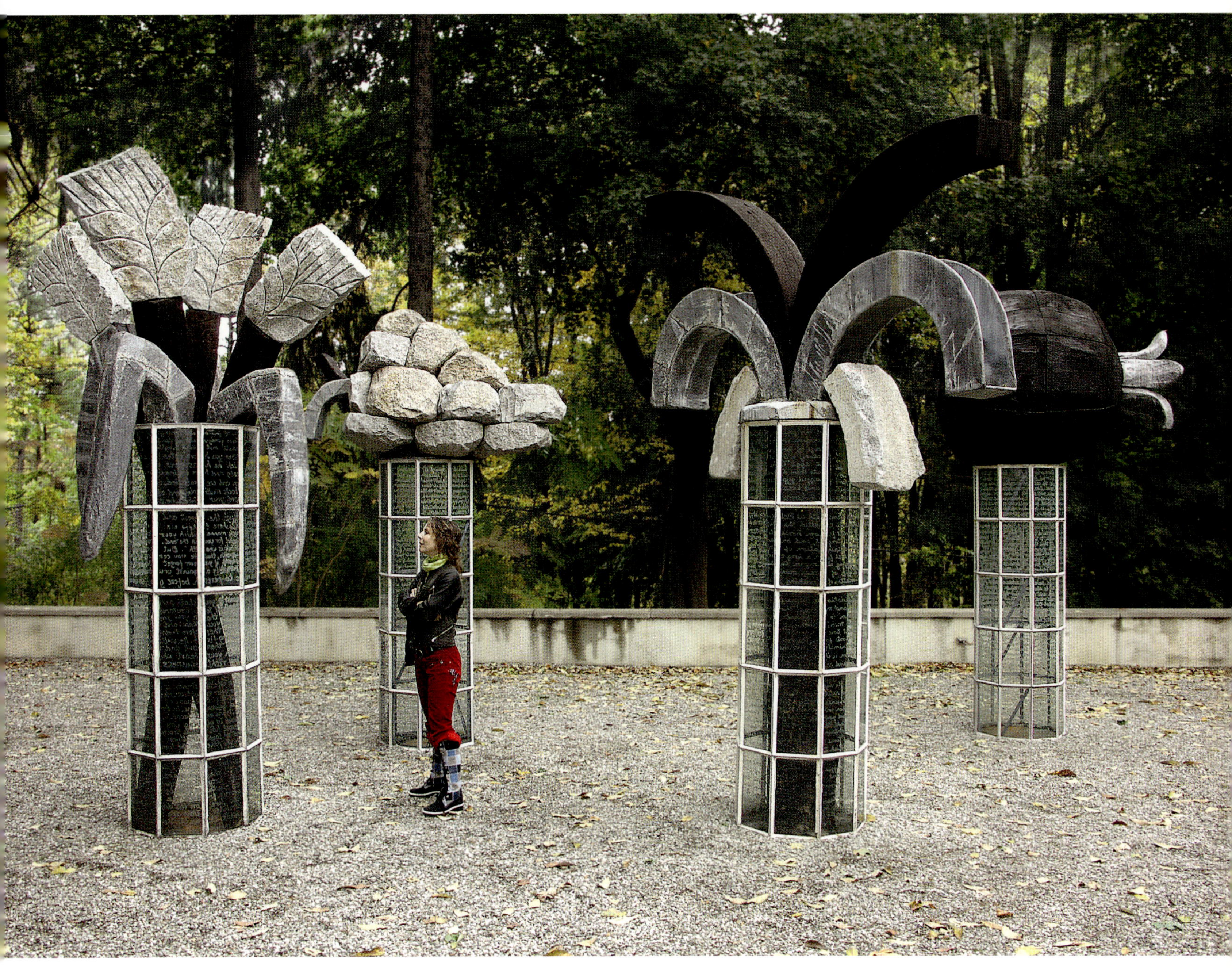

Text etched into the glass is from the following sources:
Wheat – **Deuteronomy**
Grapes – **Crime and Punishment** by Dostoyevsky
Date Palm – **One Hundred Years of Solitude** by García Márquez
Pomegranate – **The Little Prince** by Saint-Exupéry

**Skirts and Pants (after Duchamp)**, 2000
Glass, wood, steel
10 x 20 x 20 feet
On loan to the DeCordova Museum and Sculpture Park,
Lincoln, Massachusetts

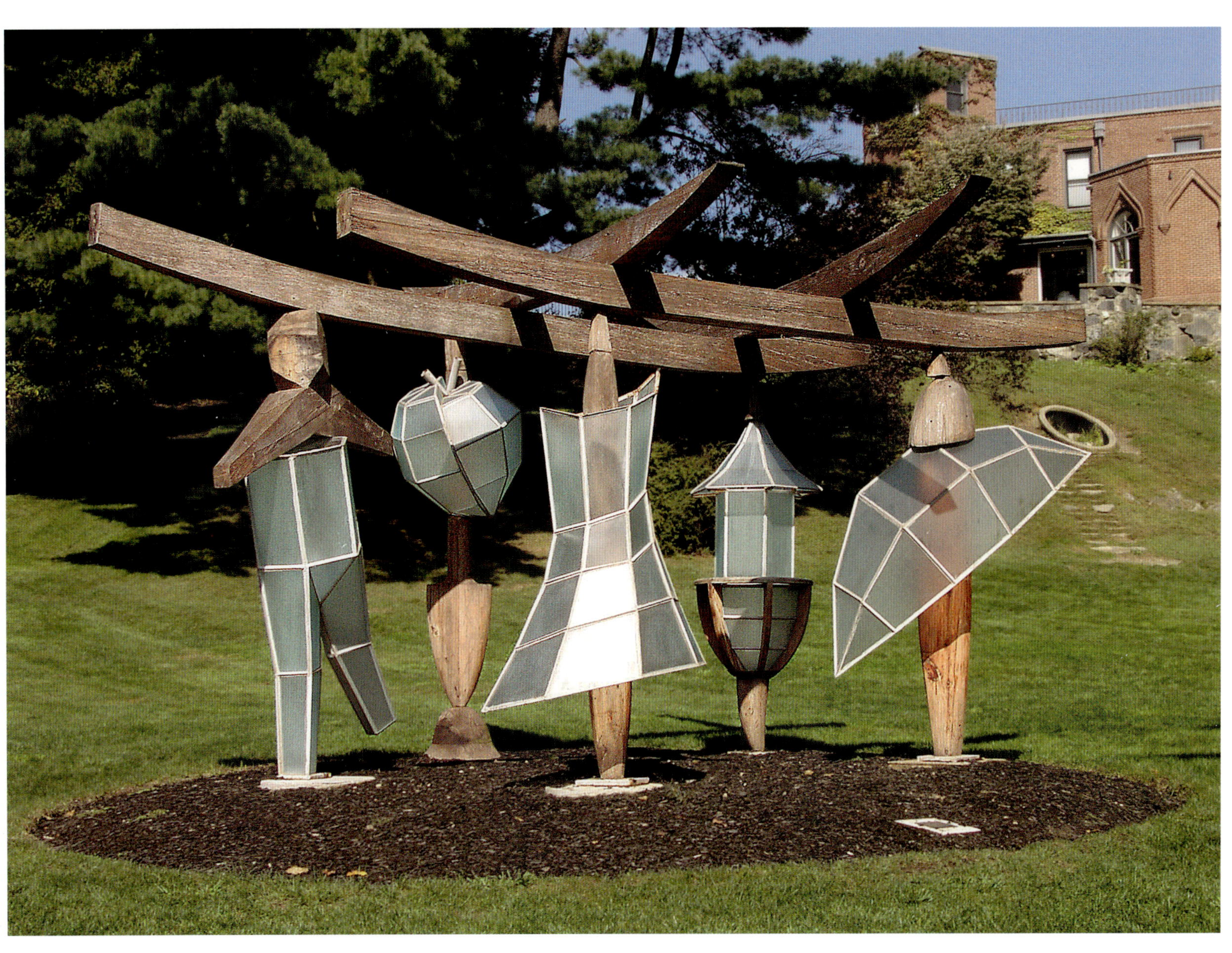

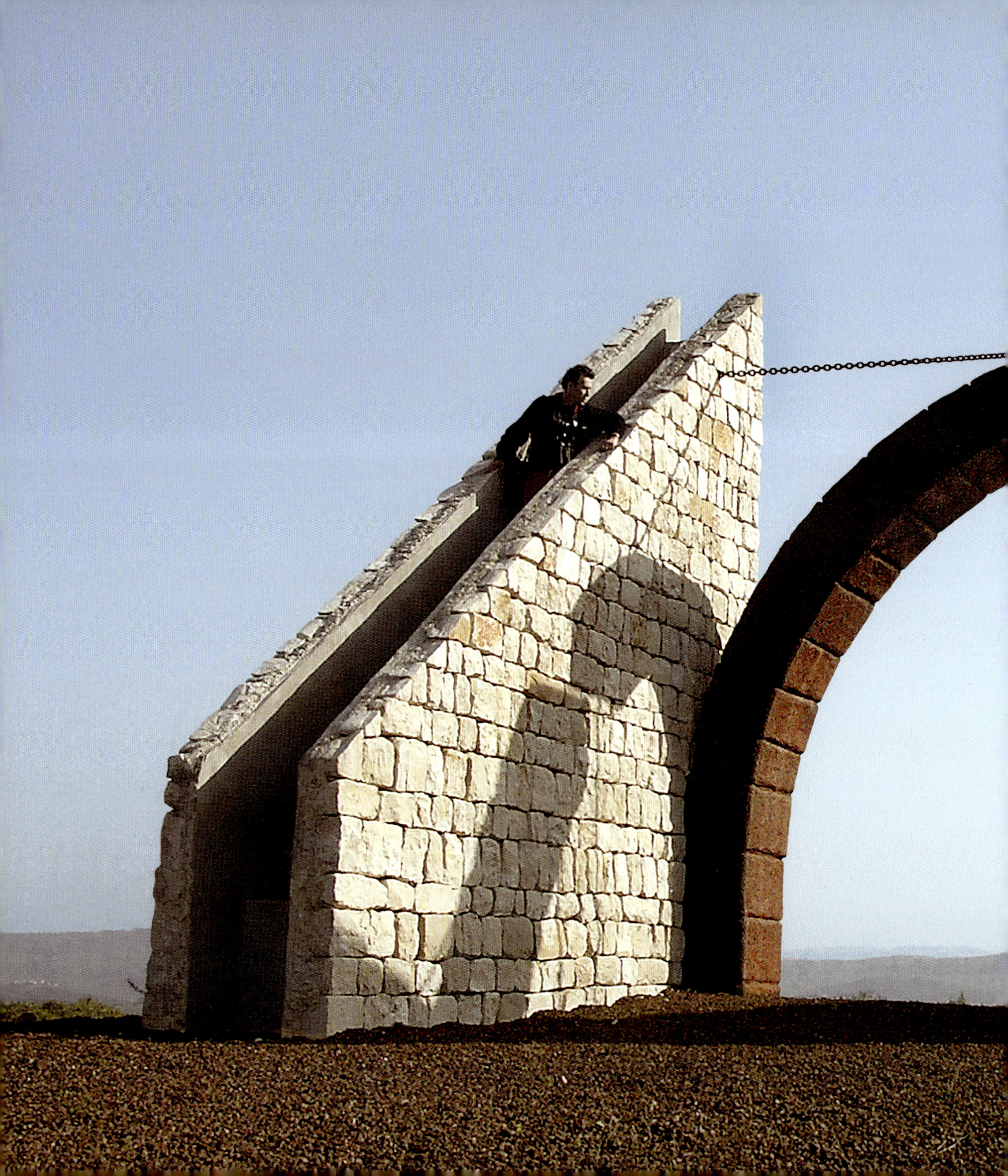

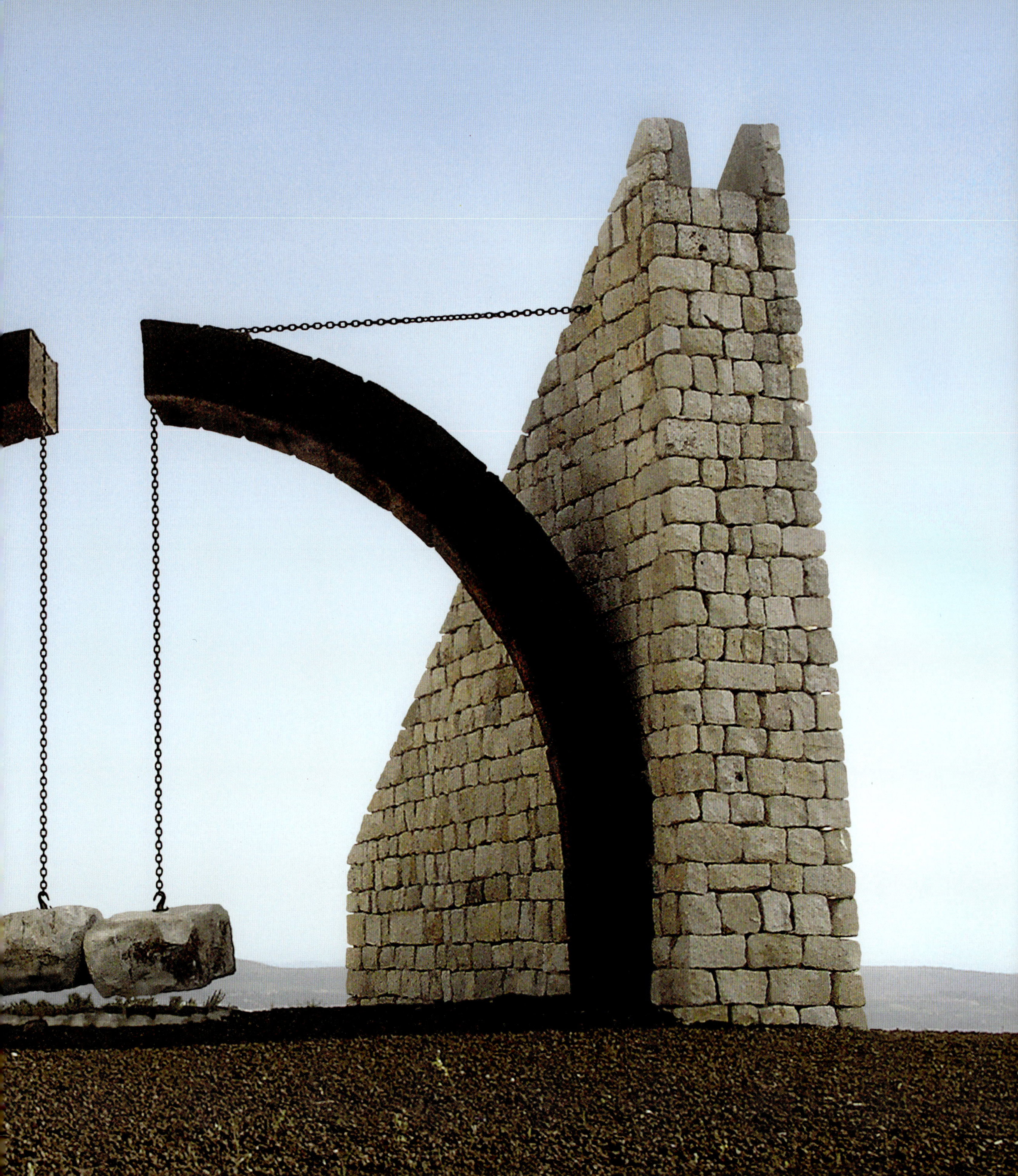

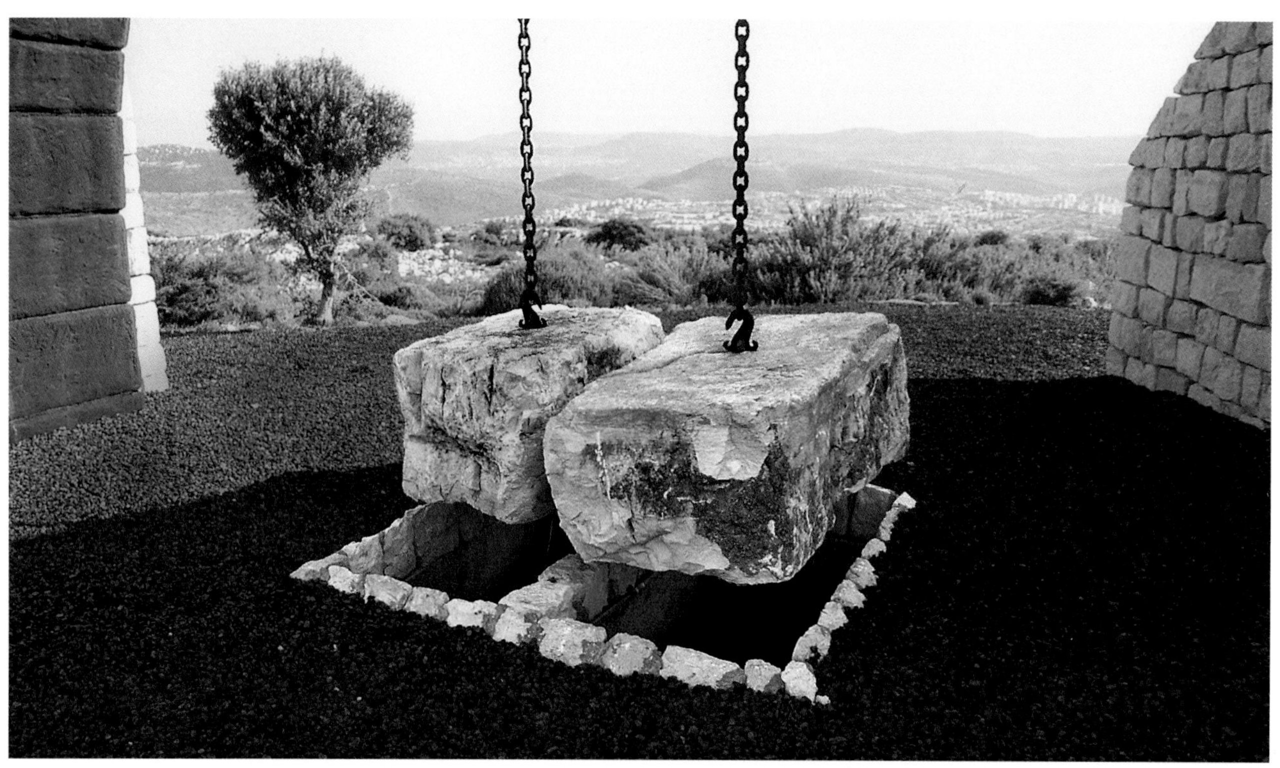

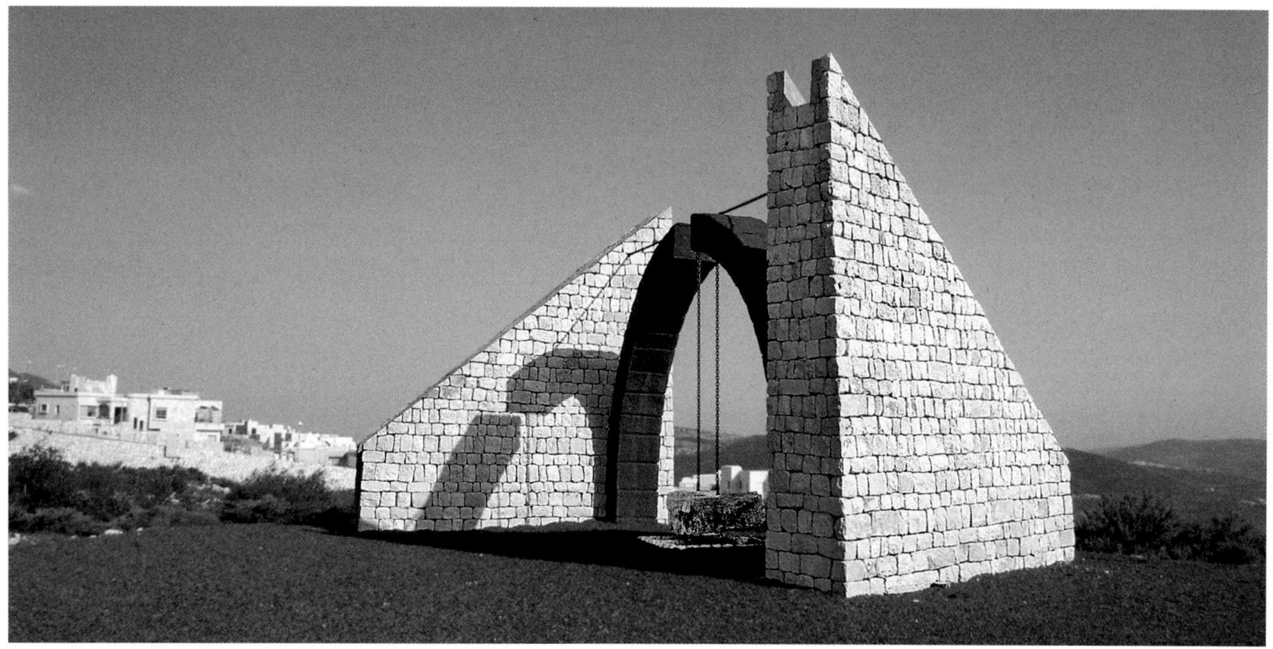

**Divided World**, *2000*
Stone, concrete, cast iron, steel, water
20 x 22 1/2 x 24 feet
Lavon, Israel
Commissioned by The Open Museum

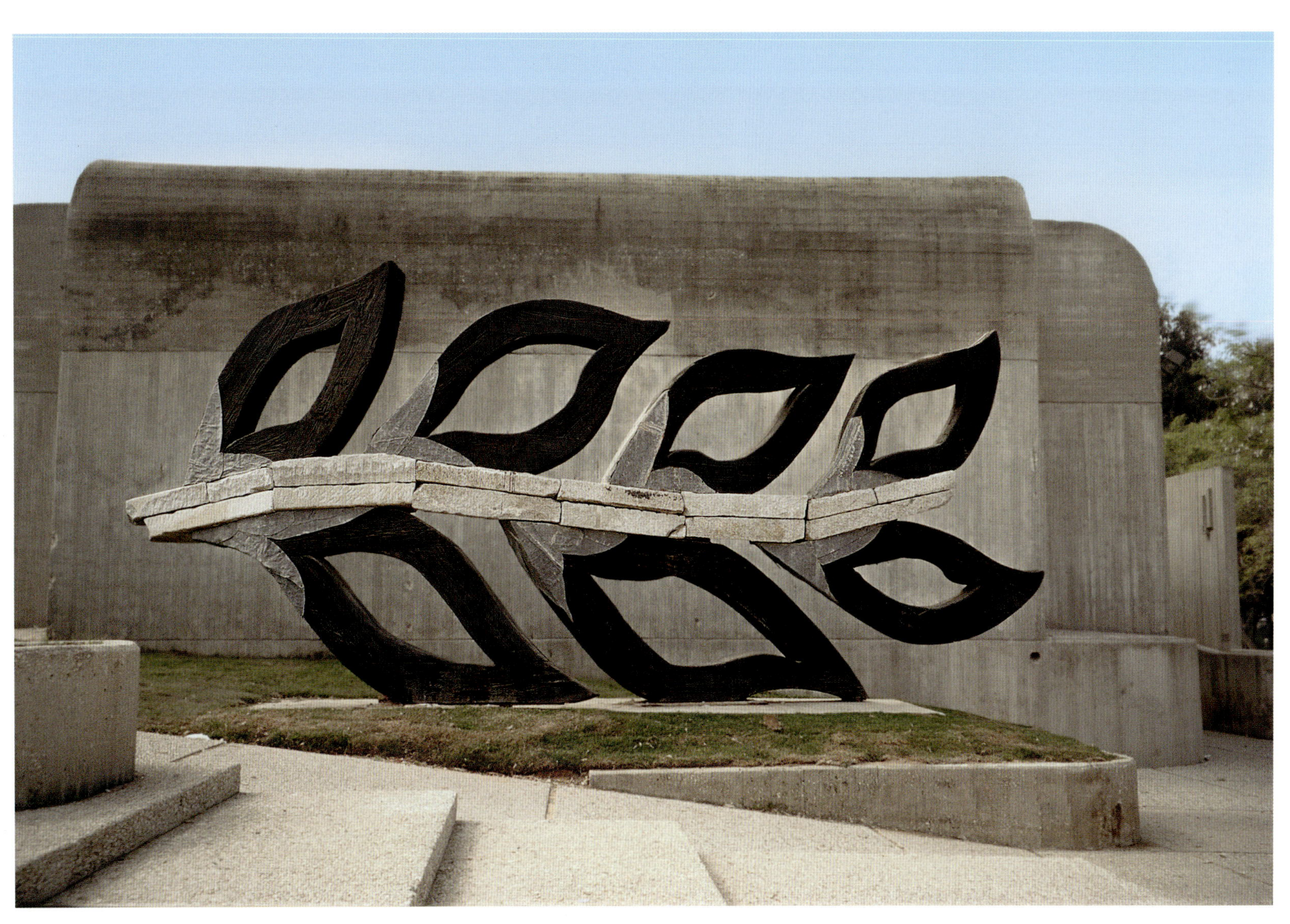

**Doubts**, 1995
Wood, stone, steel, lead
11 1/2 x 31 x 4 feet
On loan to the Herzliya Museum, Herzliya, Israel

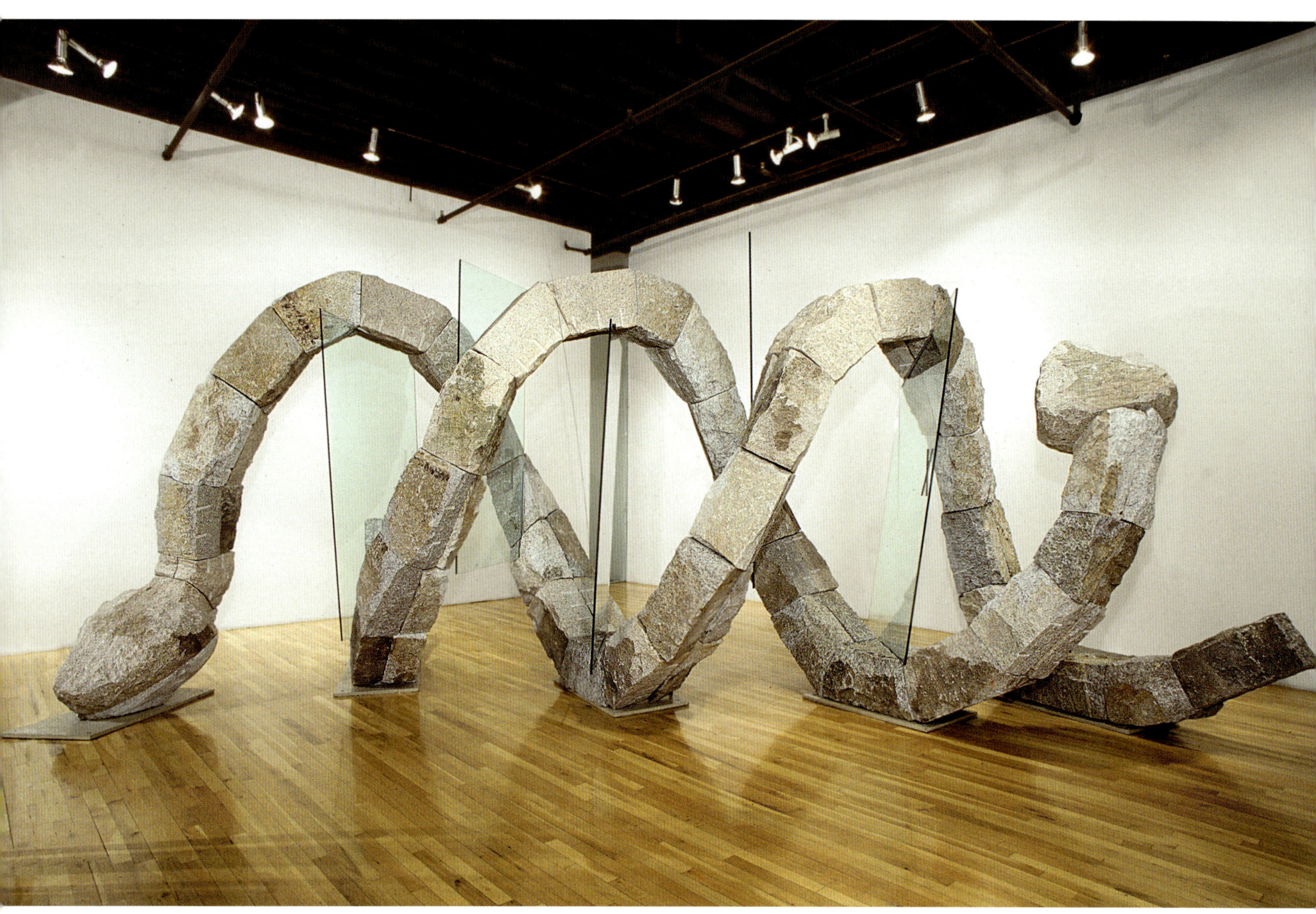

**Dream of Two Snakes**, 2002
Stone, steel, glass
9 x 21 x 6 feet
Pictured at Nancy Hoffman Gallery, New York
Messinger Collection, Harrison, New York

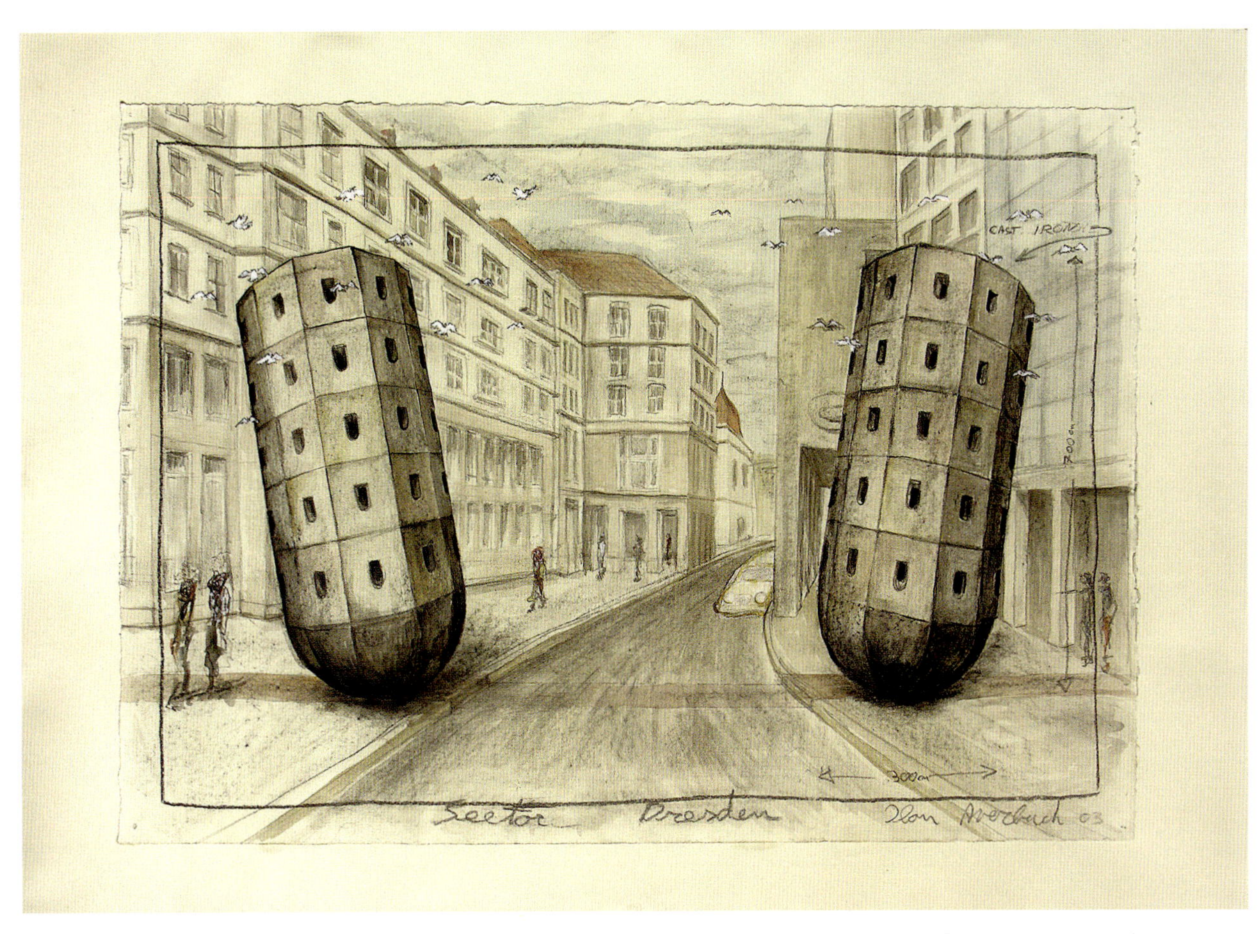

**Seetor Dresden**, 2003
Mixed media on paper
28 x 40 inches

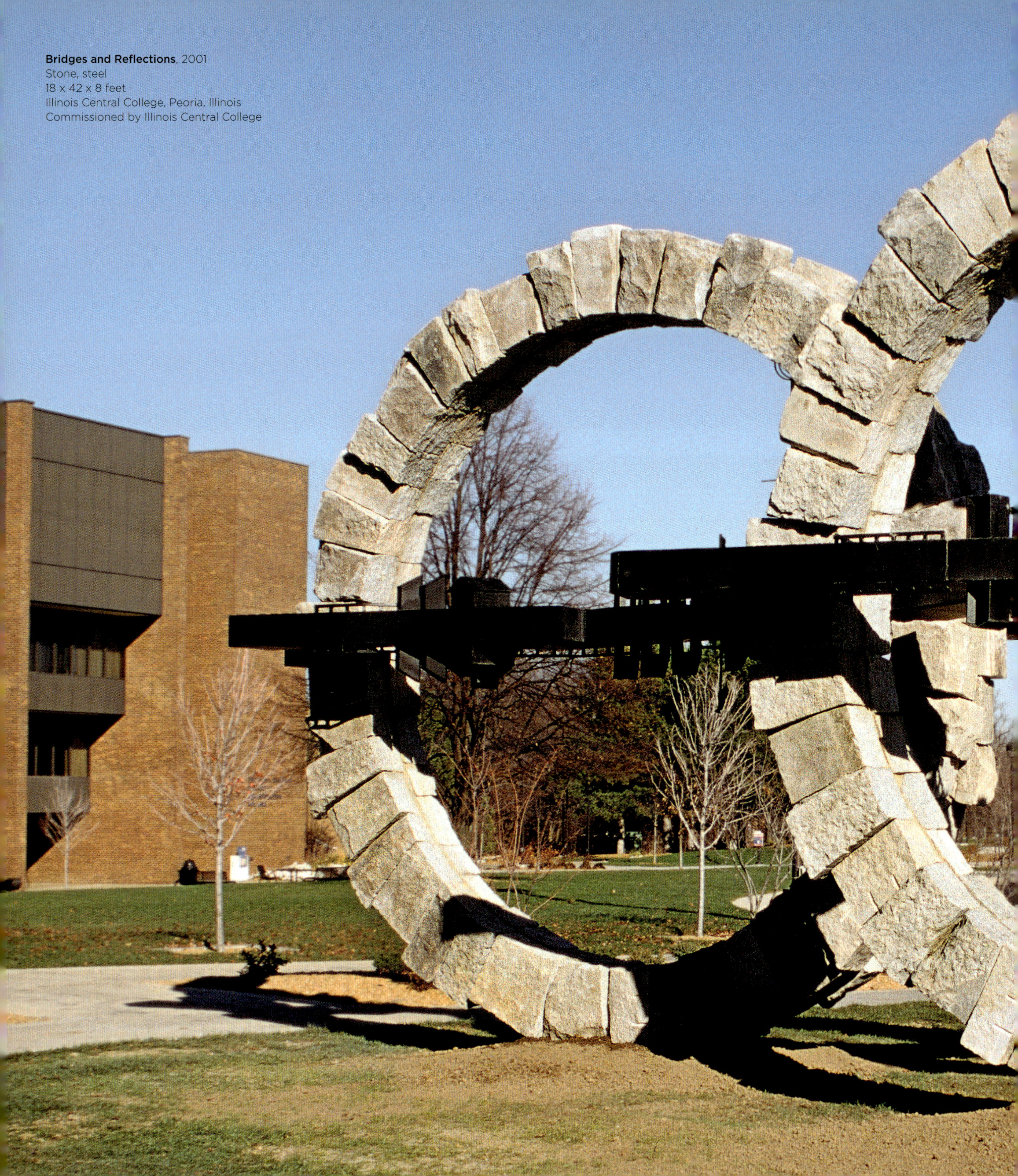


**Bridges and Reflections**, 2001
Stone, steel
18 x 42 x 8 feet
Illinois Central College, Peoria, Illinois
Commissioned by Illinois Central College

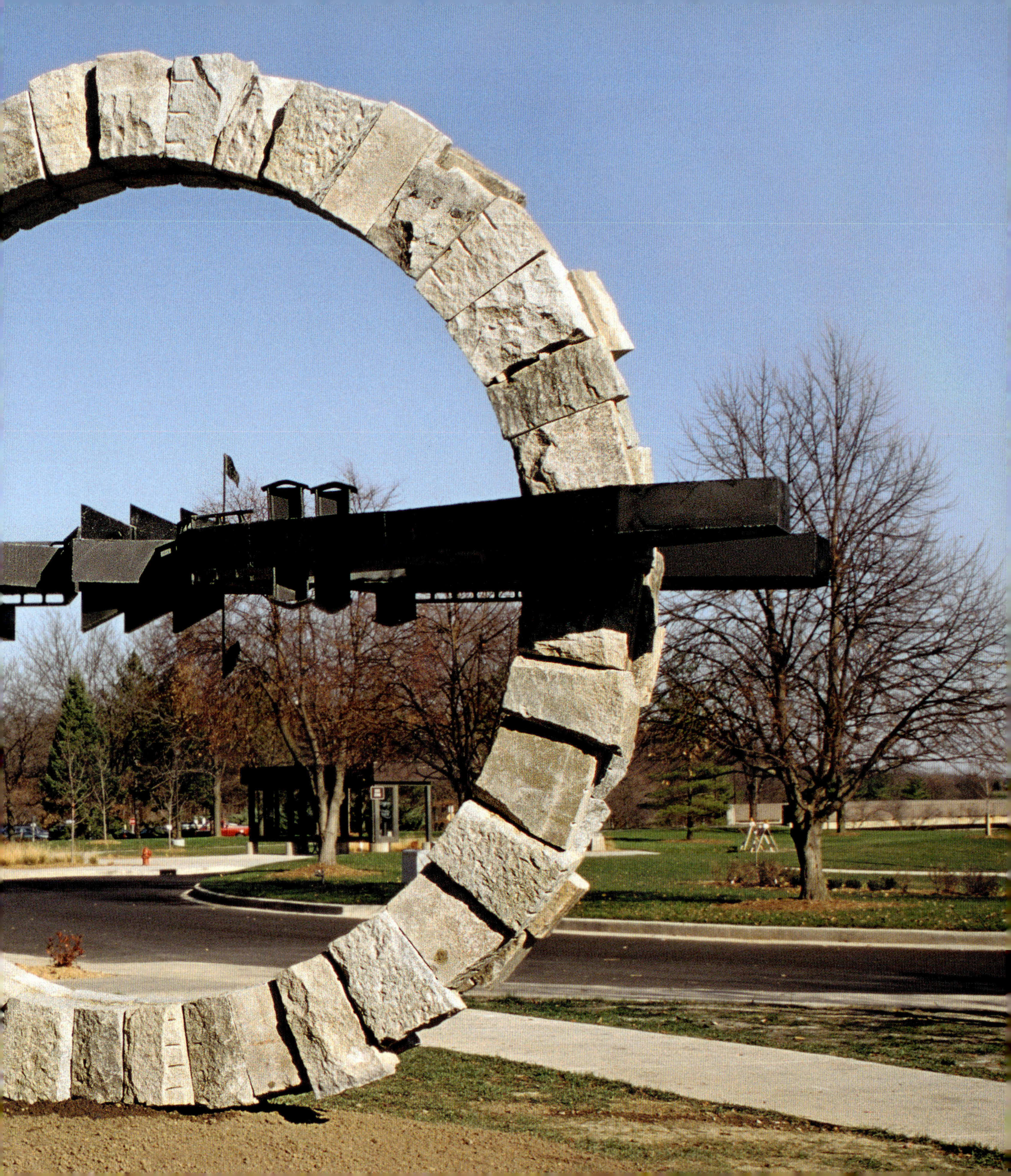

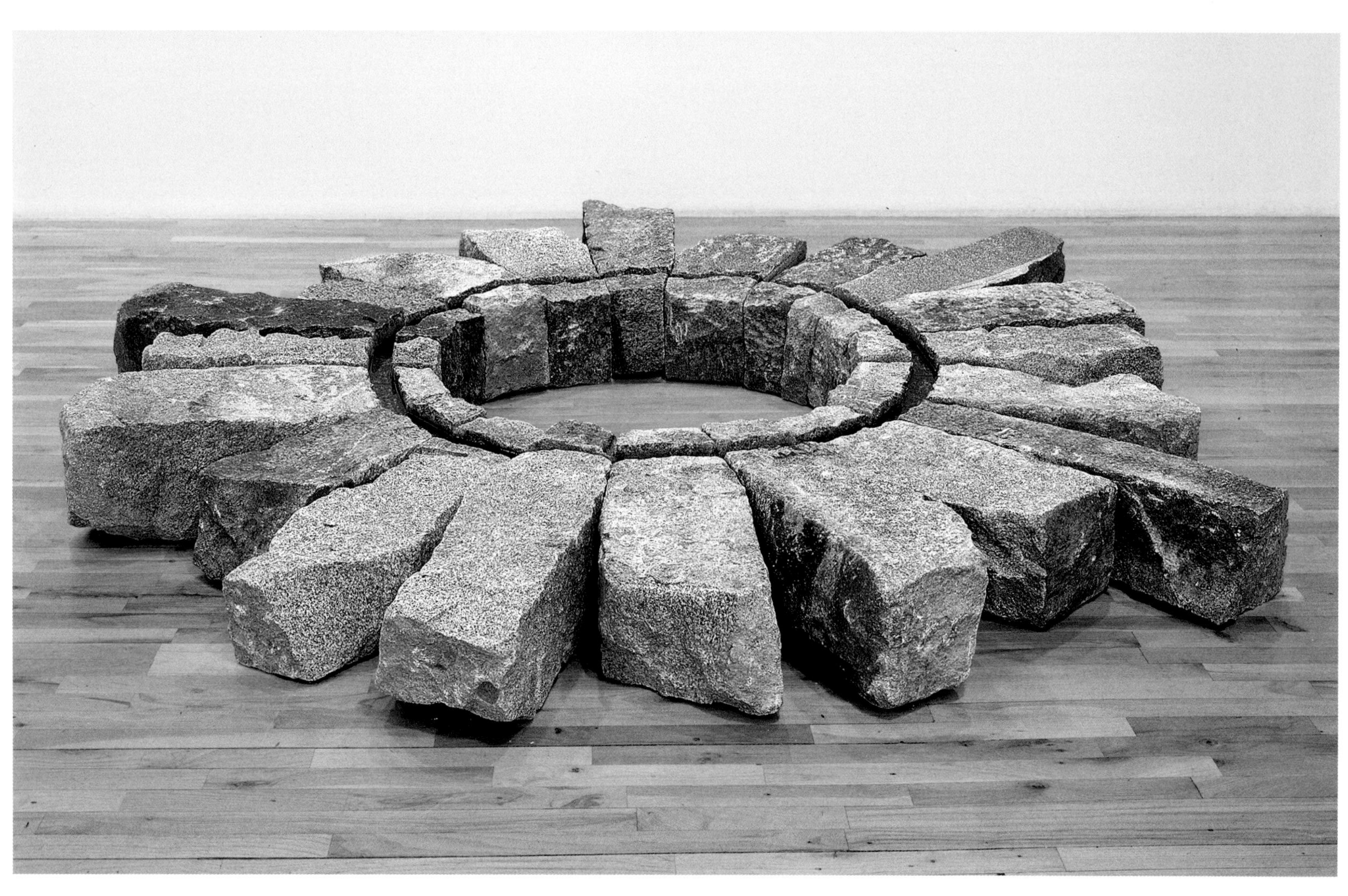

**Shadow of the Sun**, 1989
Stone, water
8 x 96 x 85 inches
Collection of the Nevada
Museum of Art, Reno, Nevada

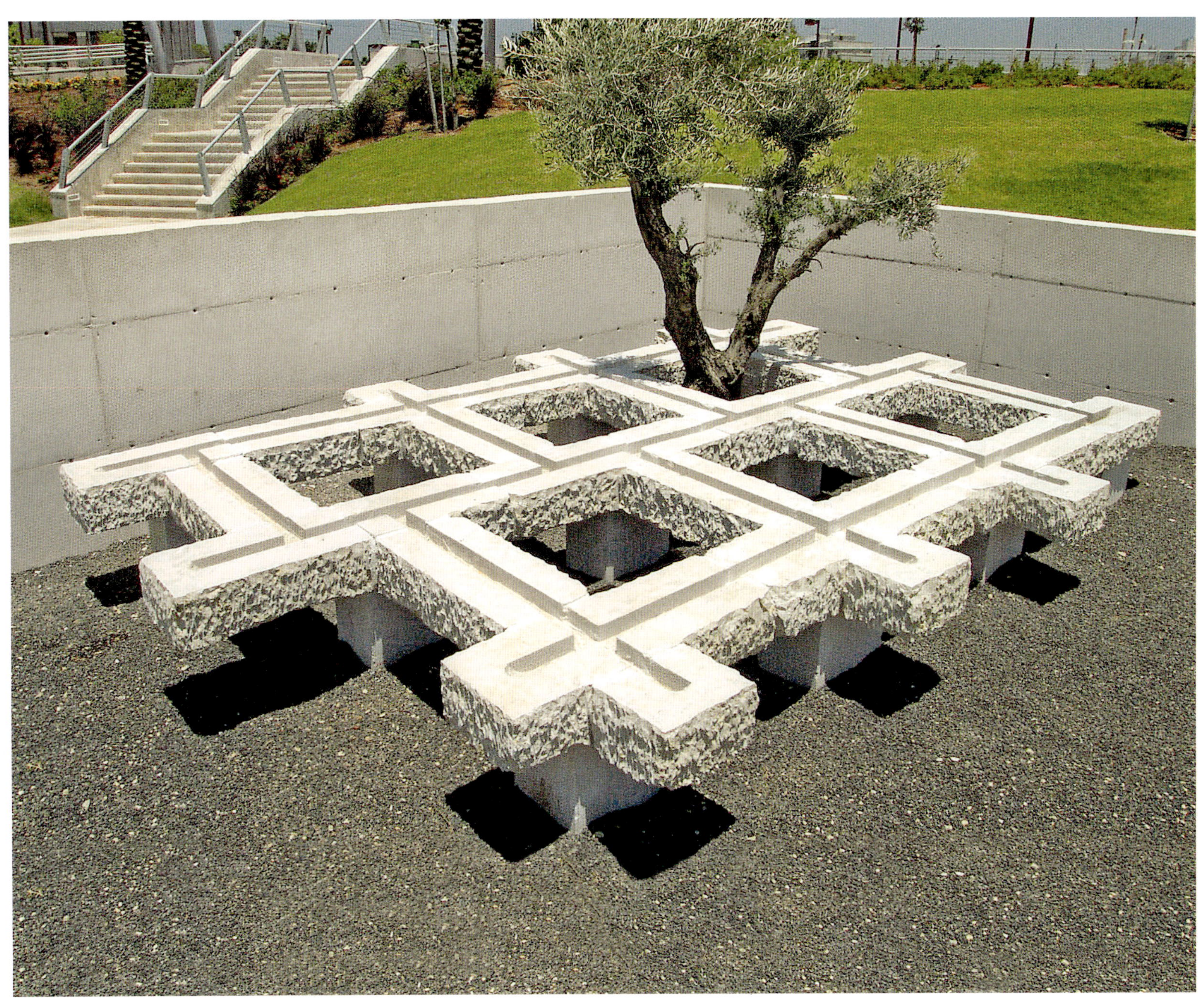

**The Game**, 2003
Stone, olive tree
8 x 21 x 15 feet
Commissioned by Bar Ilan University, Israel

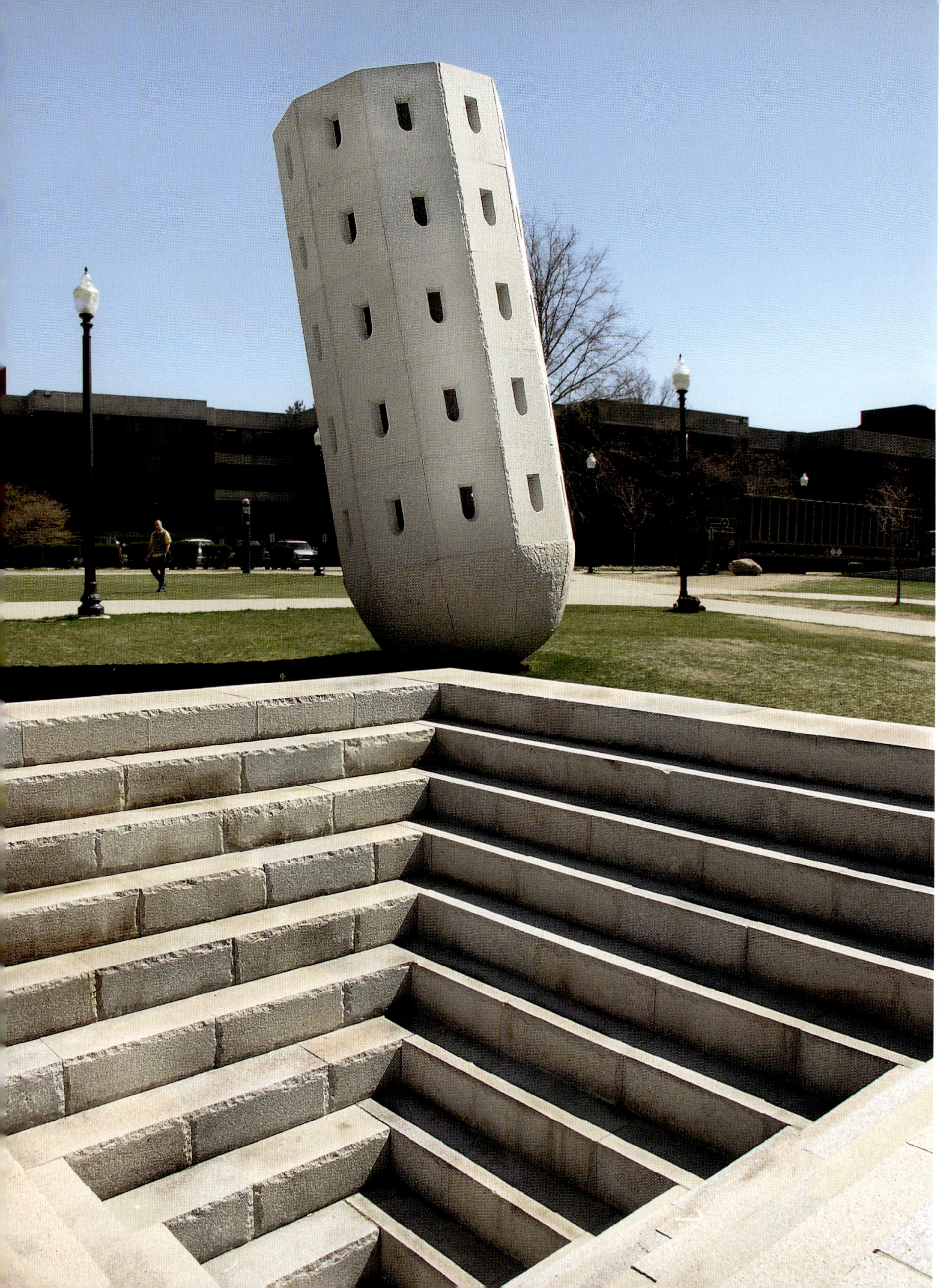

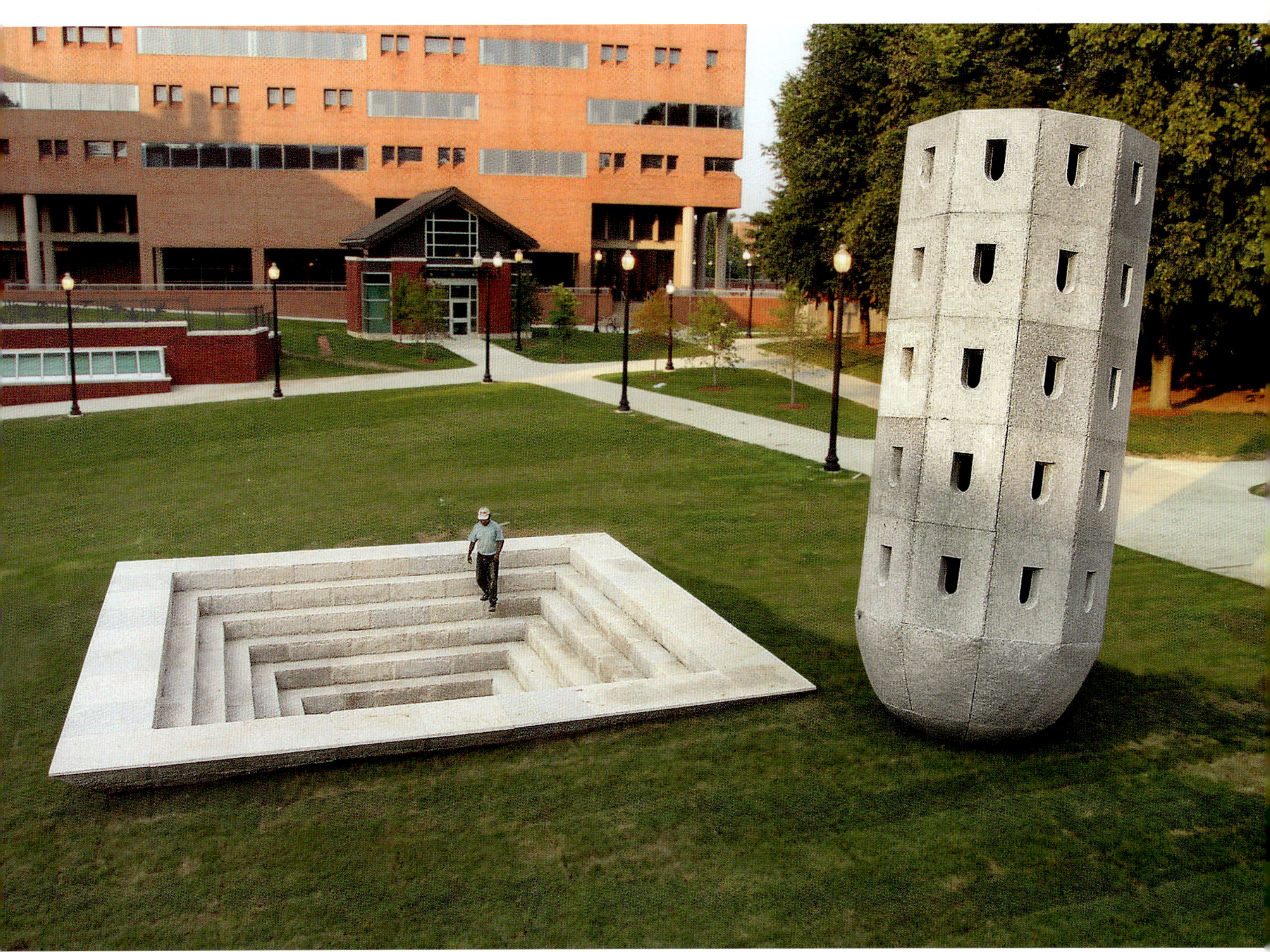

**The Dove Tower and Steps
to the Bottom of a Pyramid**, 2004
Stone
22 x 39 x 48 feet
The University of Connecticut at Storrs
Commissioned by the CT Commission on
Culture and Tourism

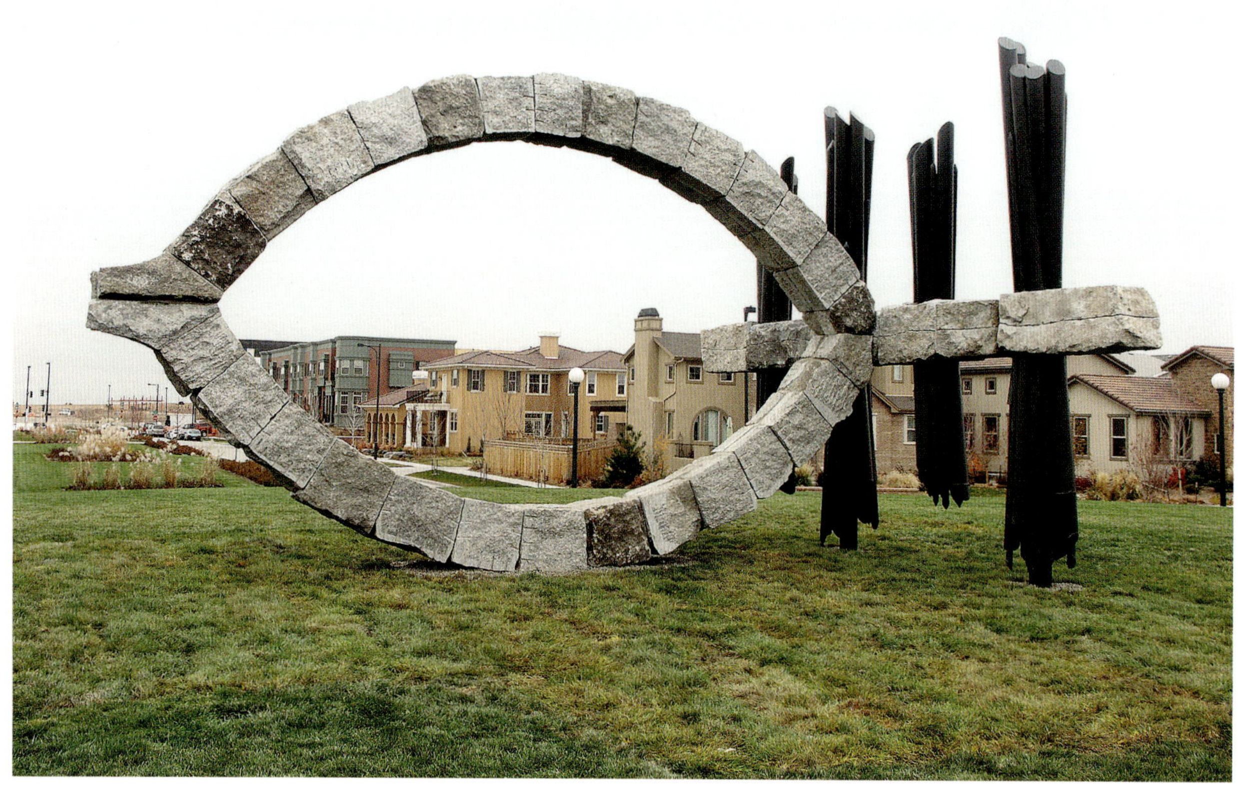

**The Eye and the Horizon (after Monet),** 2006
Stone, steel
16 x 27 x 23 feet
Stapleton, Denver, Colorado
Commissioned by Park Creek Metropolitan District

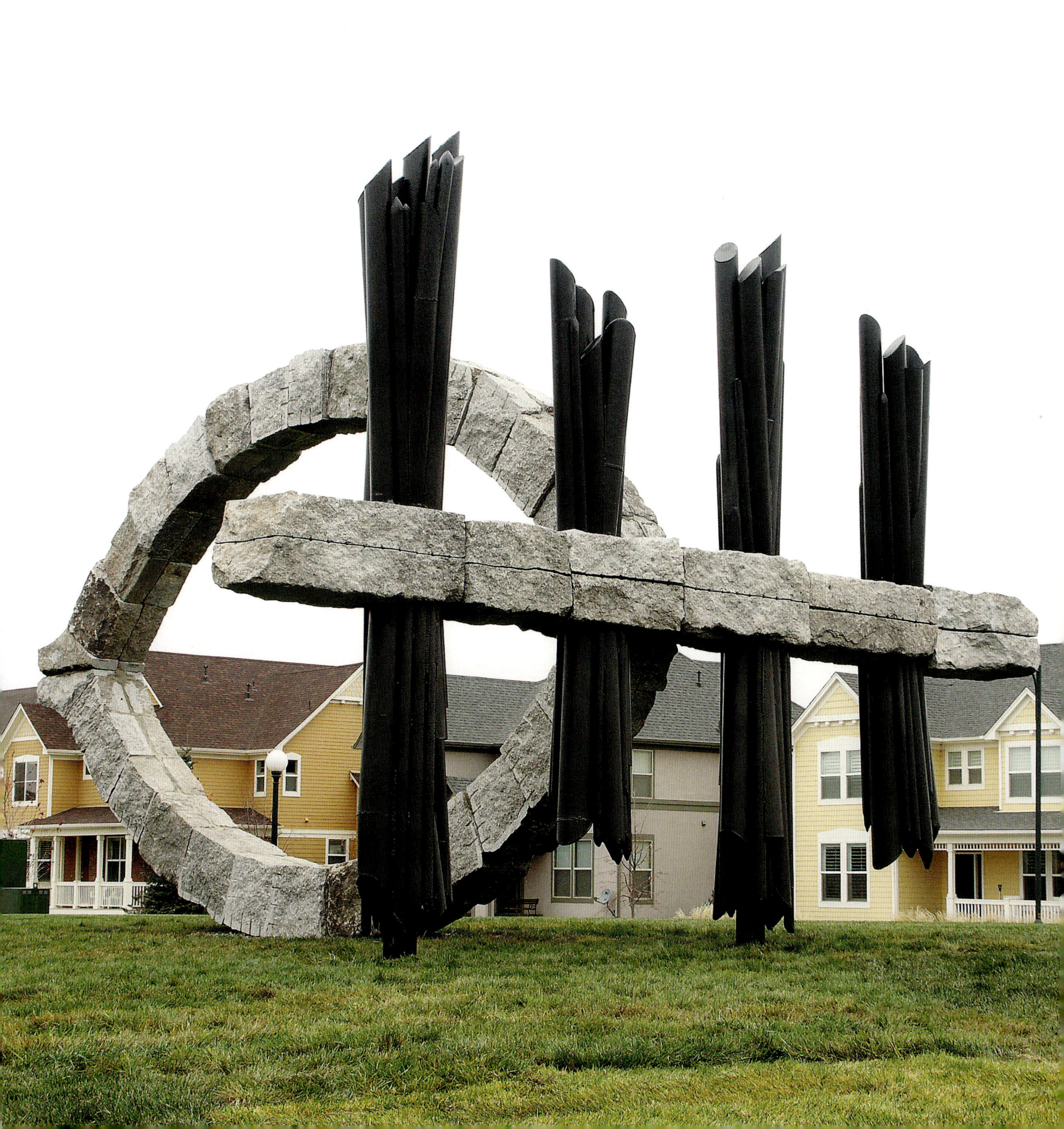

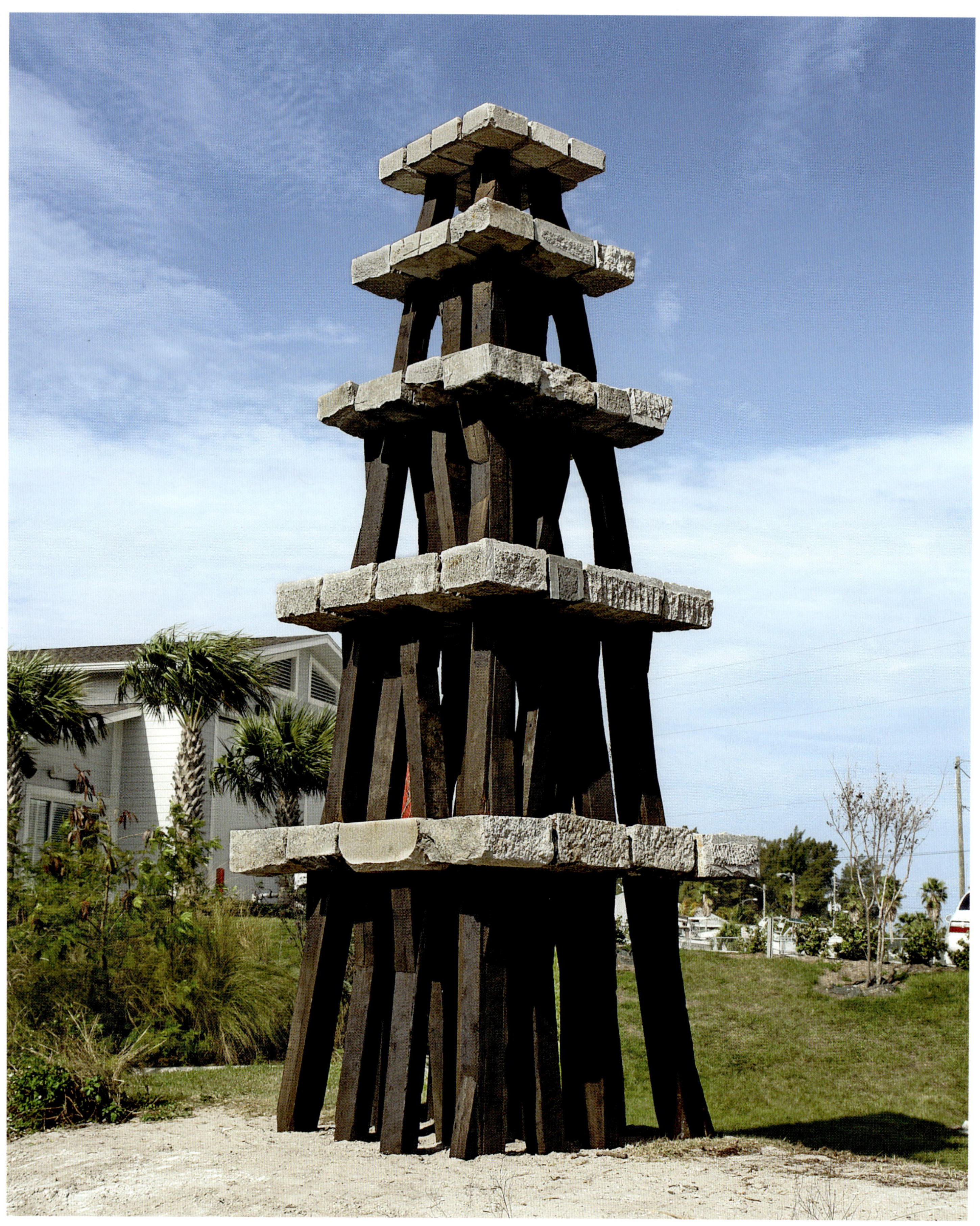

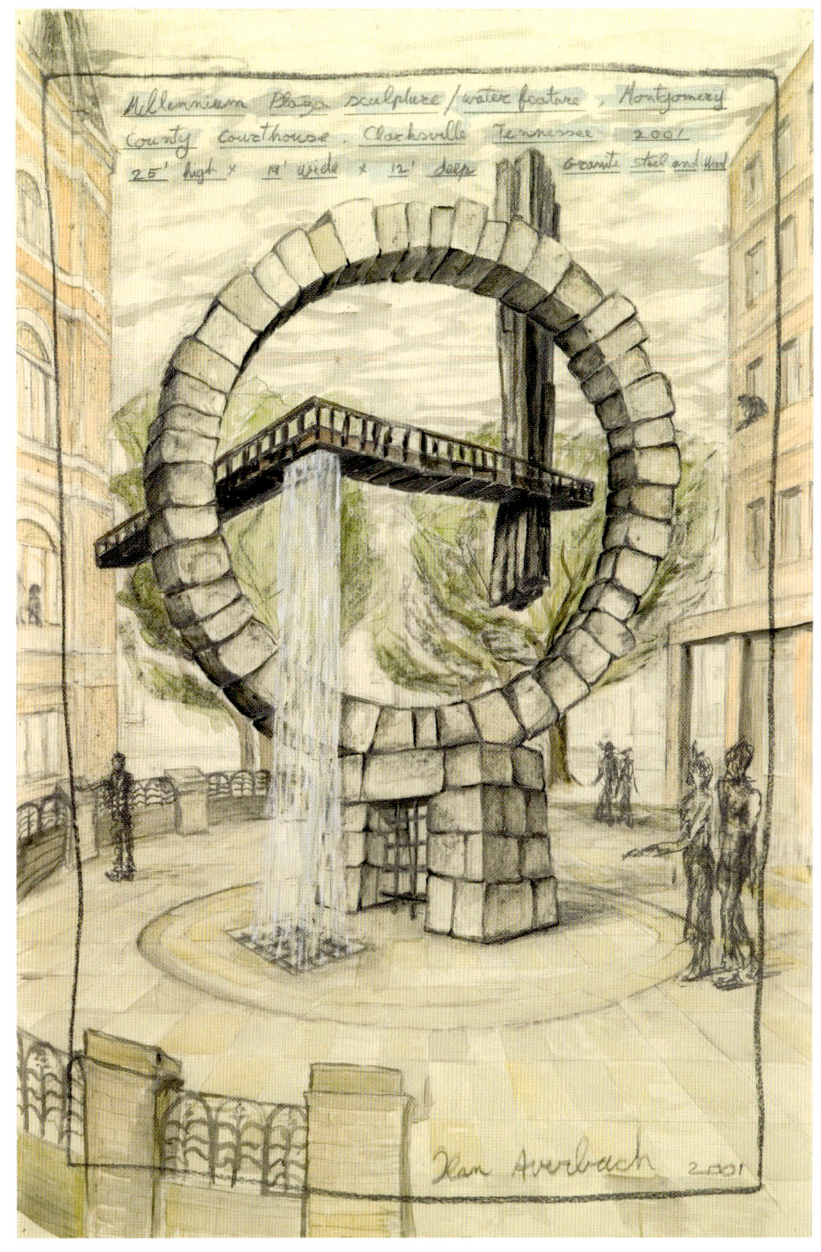


**Layers**, 2006
Stone, steel, wood
22 x 8 x 8 feet
Fire Station #2, Tierra Verde, Florida
Commissioned by the Pinellas County Arts
Council

**Hurricane**, 2001
Mixed media on paper
44 x 30 inches

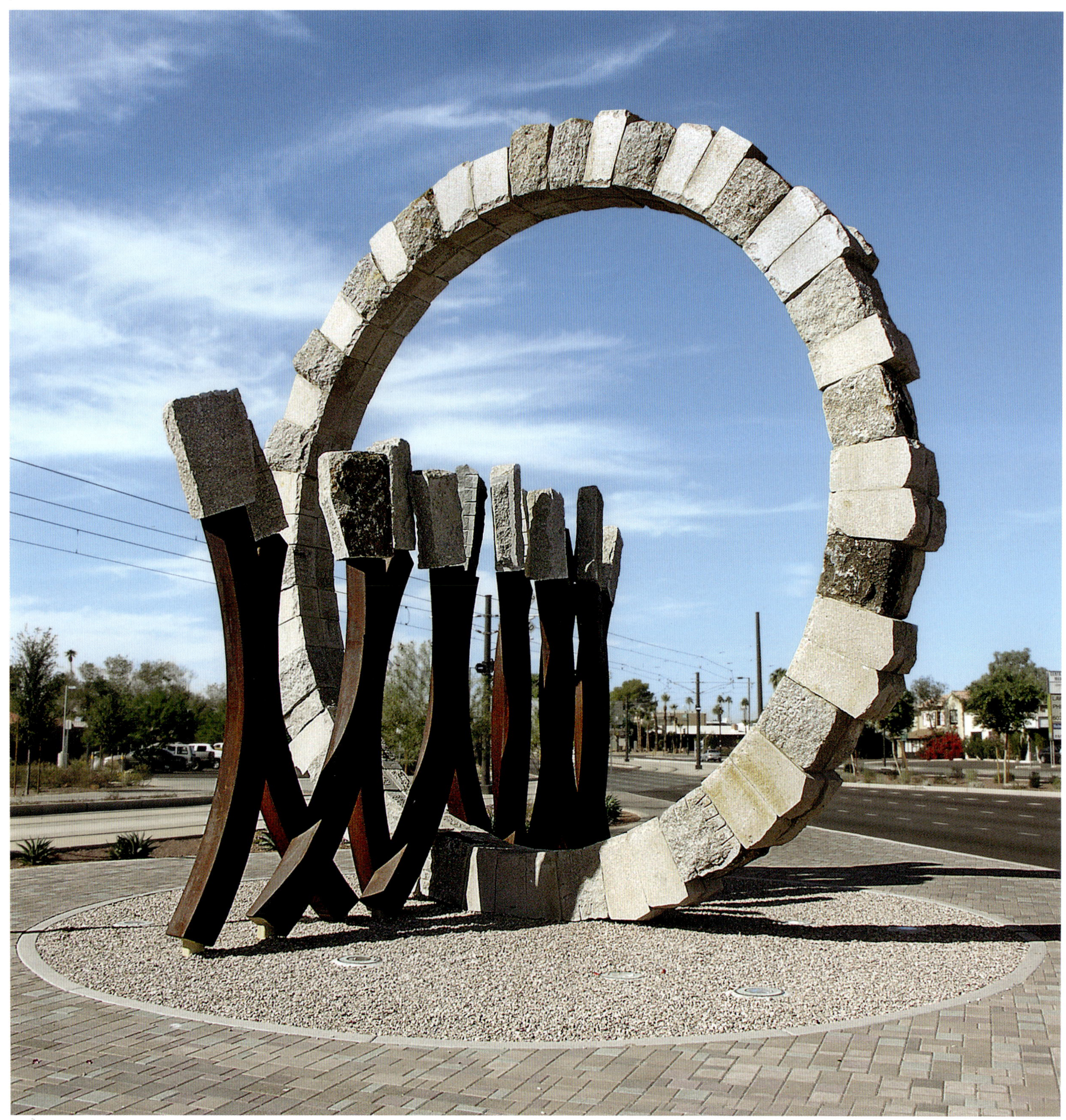

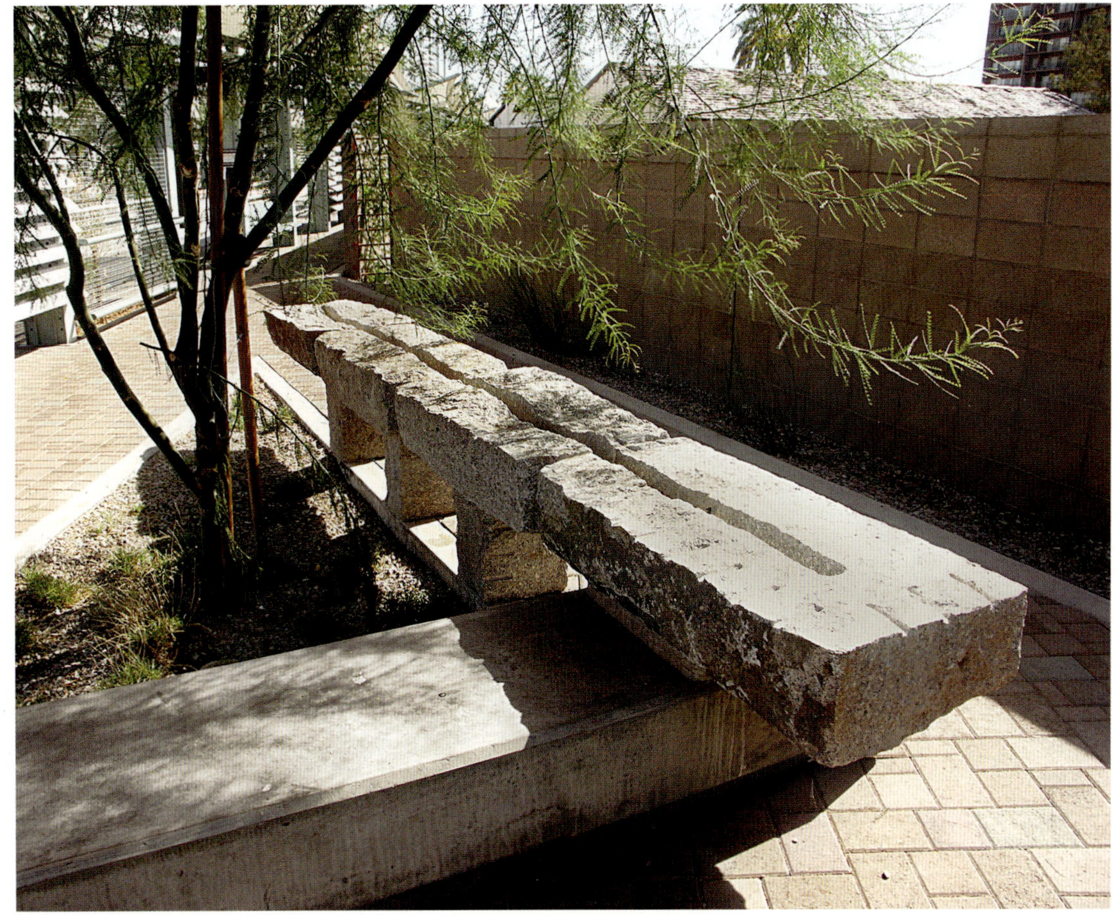

**Landmark (The Crossing)**, 2008
Stone, steel
24 x 24 x 22 feet
Camelback Transit Center, Phoenix, Arizona
Commissioned by Valley Metro Rail

**Trough Seat and Tree**, 2008
Stone, concrete, plumbing, tree
2 1/2 x 18 x 8 1/2 feet, one on each of two station platforms
Camelback Transit Center, Phoenix, Arizona
Commissioned by Valley Metro Rail

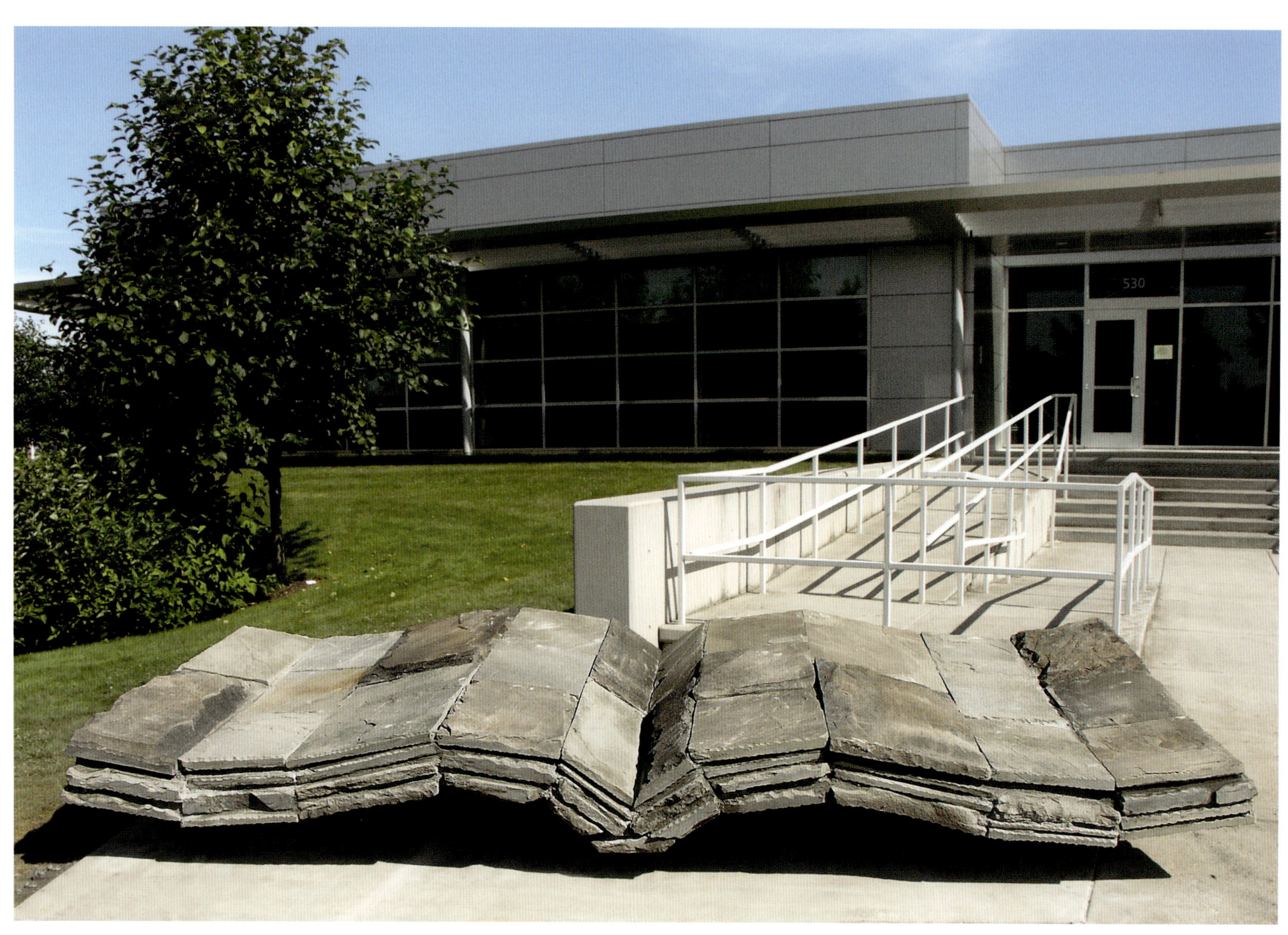

**The Book**, 2009
Stone, steel
2 x 14 x 7 feet
Oregon State Data Center, Salem, Oregon
Collection of the State of Oregon

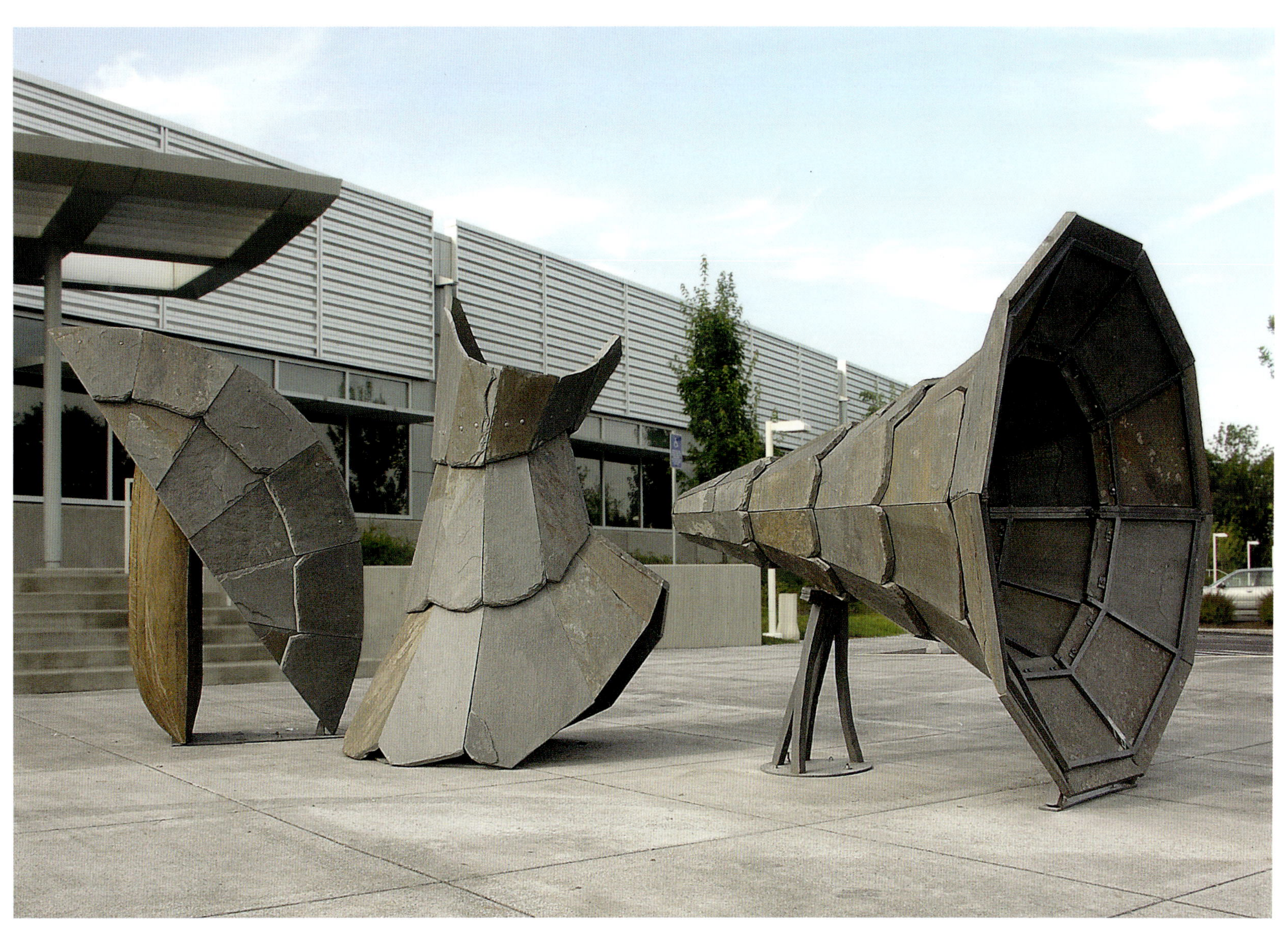

**The Dress, the Voice, and the Bachelor's Coat**, 2005
Stone, steel, wood
8 x 24 x 8 feet
Oregon State Data Center, Salem, Oregon
Collection of the State of Oregon

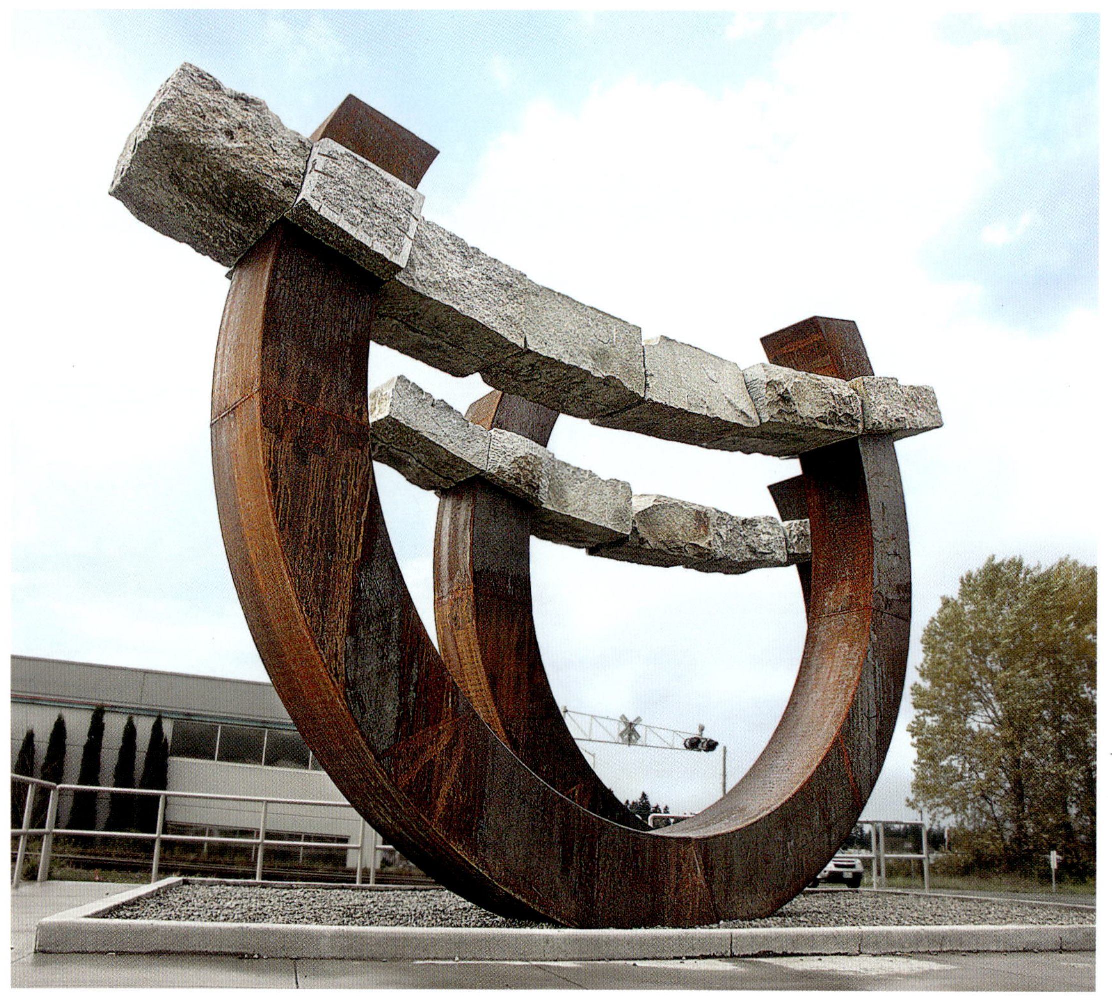

**South Tacoma**, 2008
Stone, steel
18 x 37 x 11 feet
South Tacoma commuter rail station,
Tacoma, Washington
Commissioned by Sound Transit

**End of the Line**, 2008
Stone
8 x 4 feet x length of the station
South Tacoma commuter rail station, Tacoma, Washington
Commissioned by Sound Transit

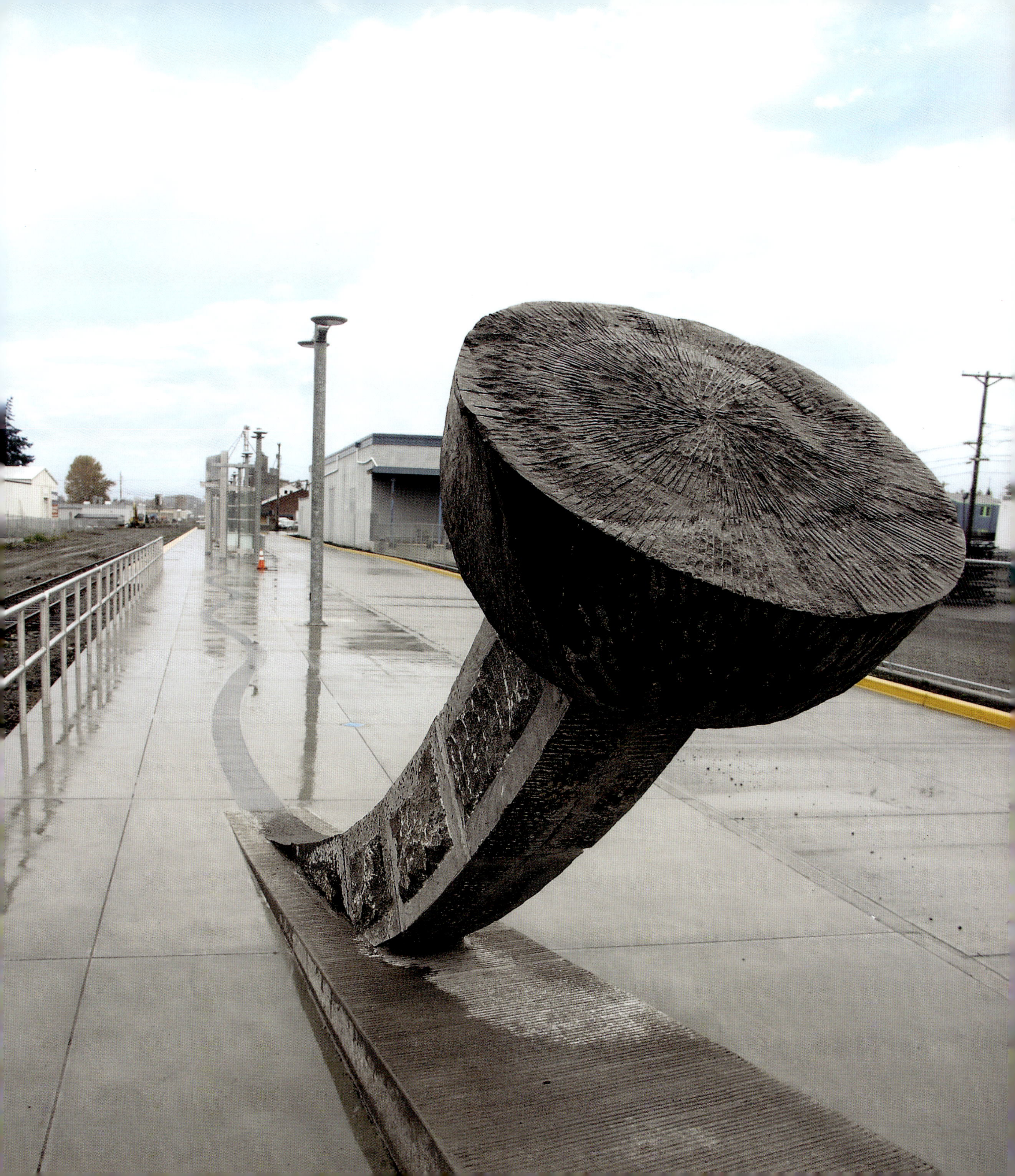

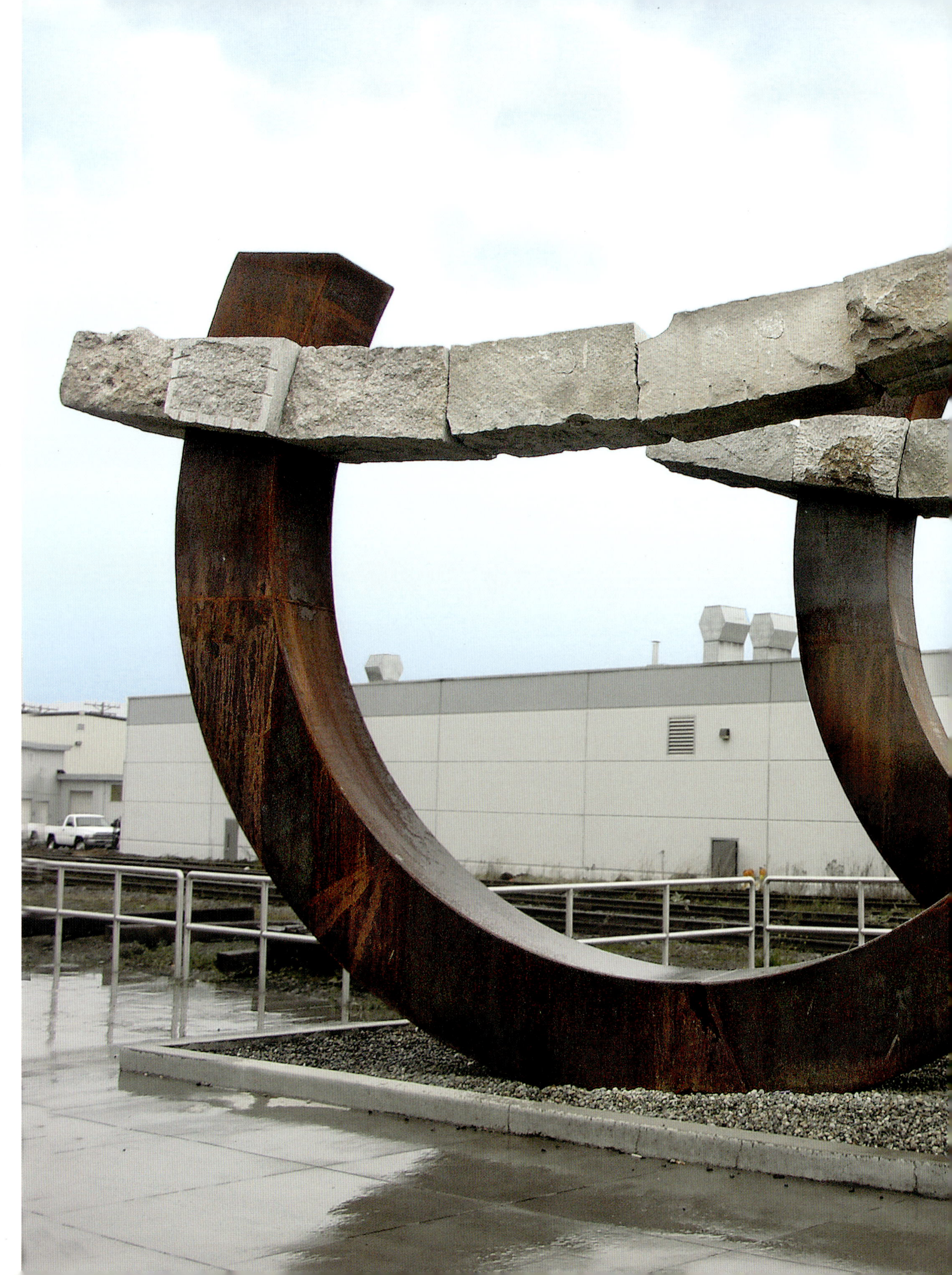

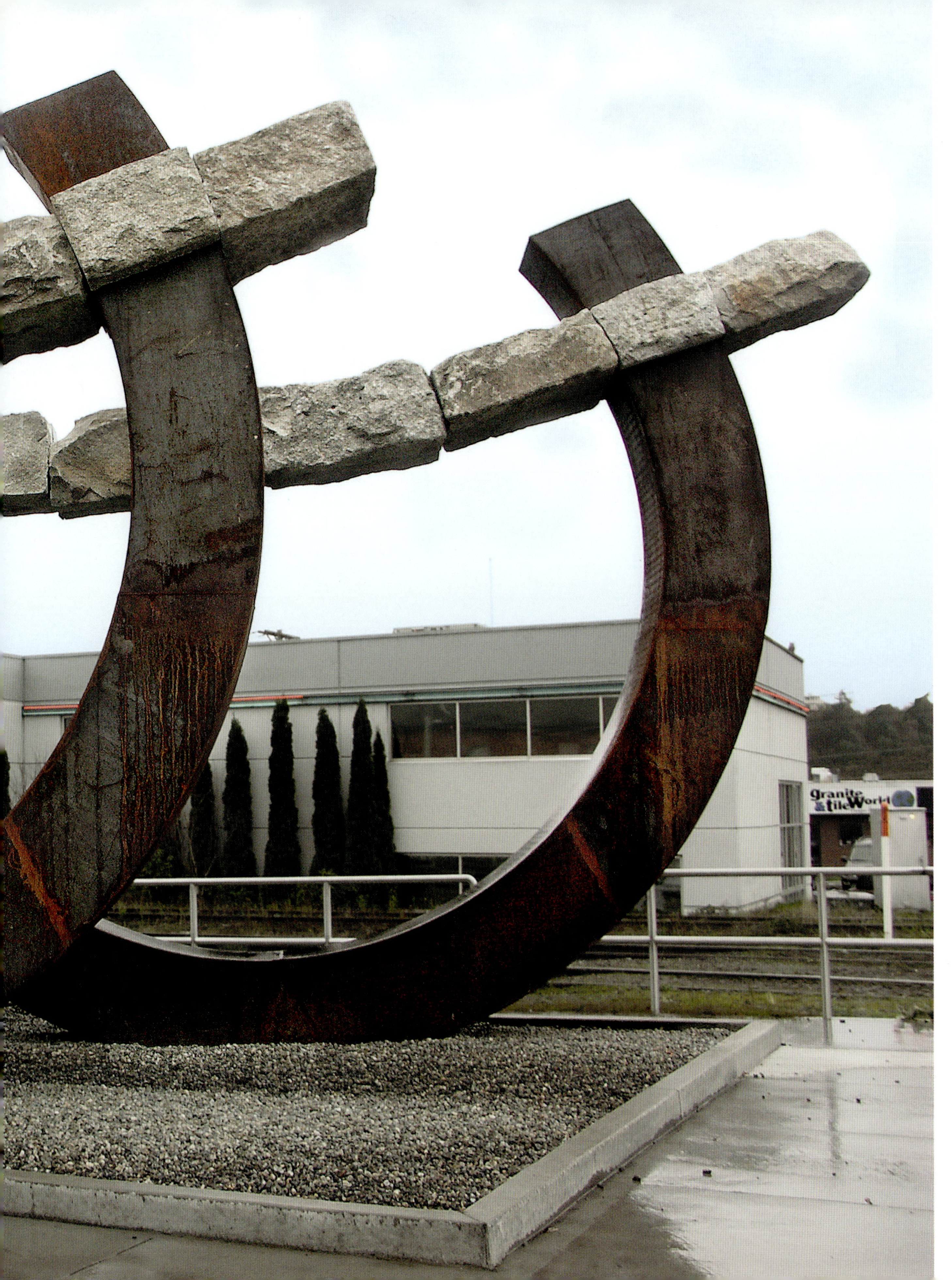

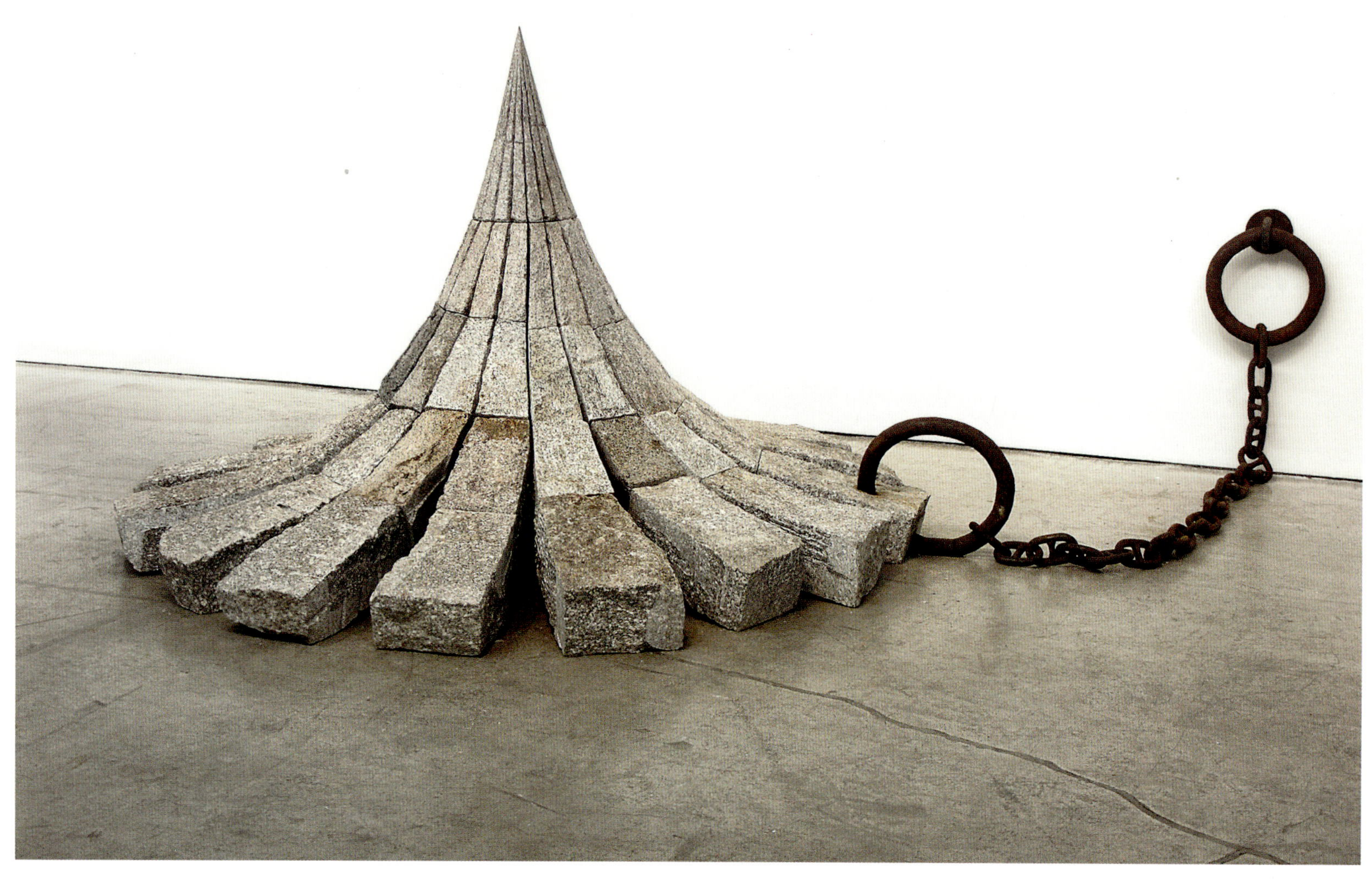

**Tumbleweed**, 2008
Stone, steel
66 x 112 x 184 inches

**Self-Portrait**, 2008
Steel, lead, glass
13 x 15 x 11 feet

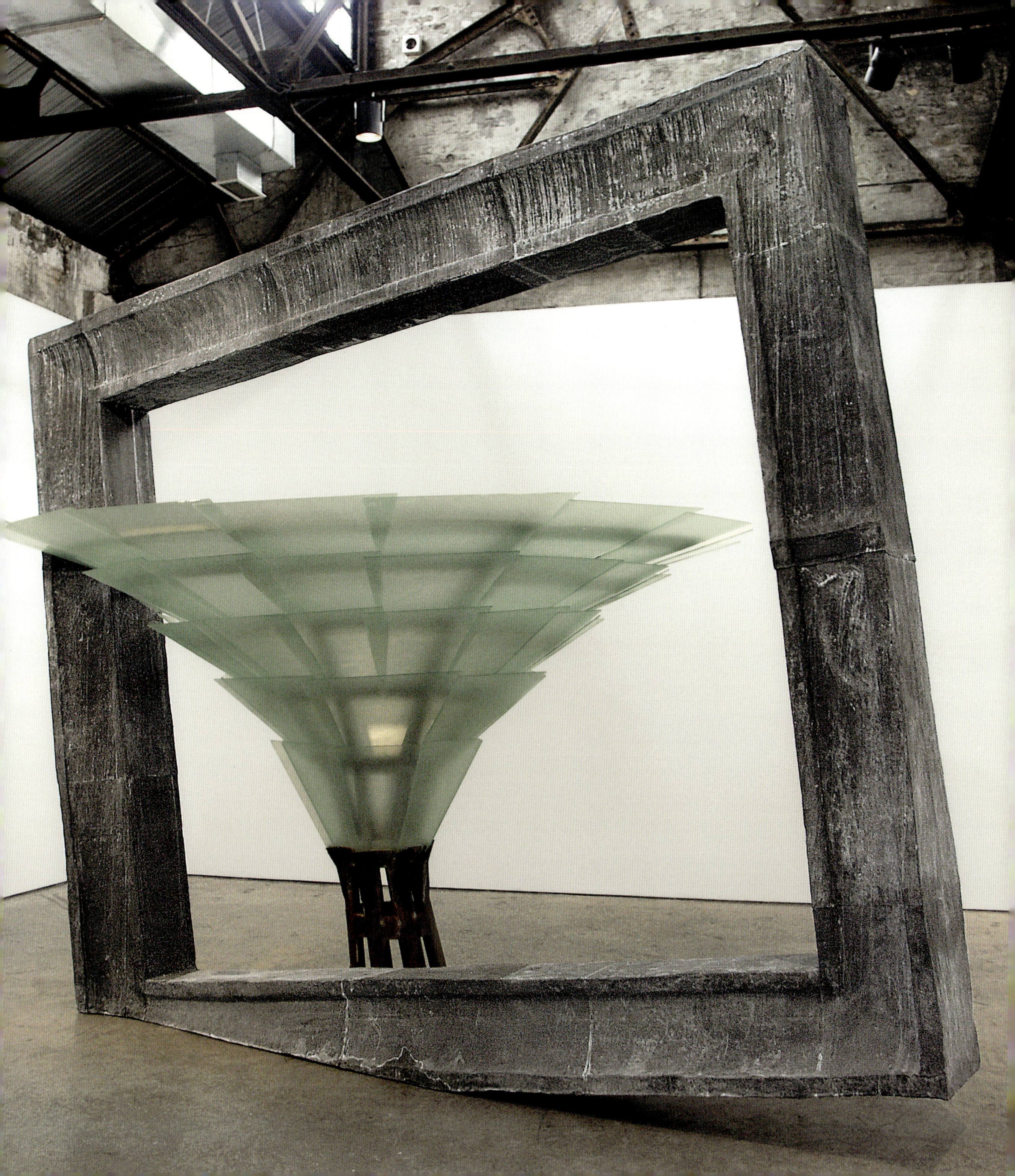

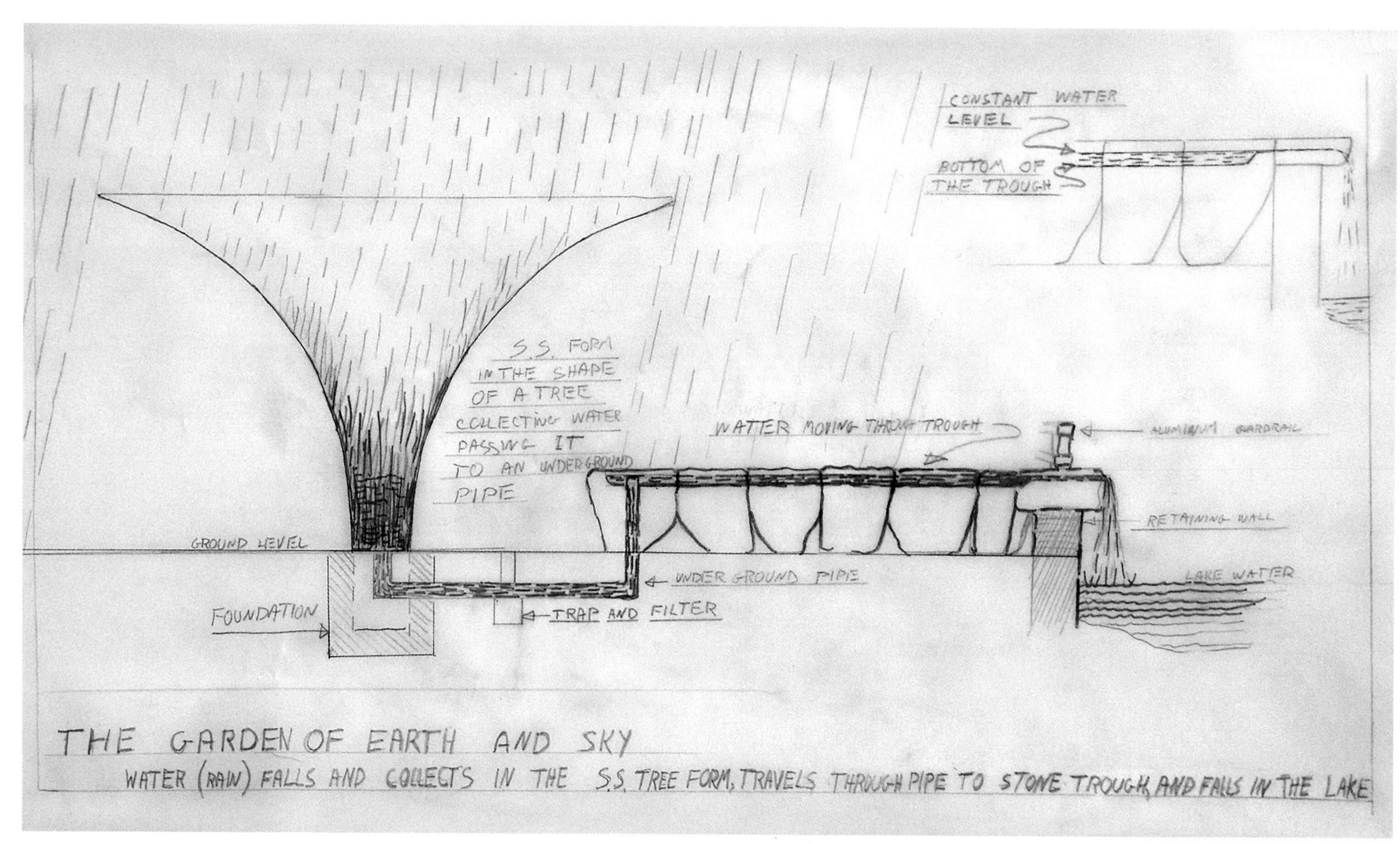


**Schematic for Water, the Garden of Earth and Sky**, 2009
Mixed media on paper
14 x 25 inches

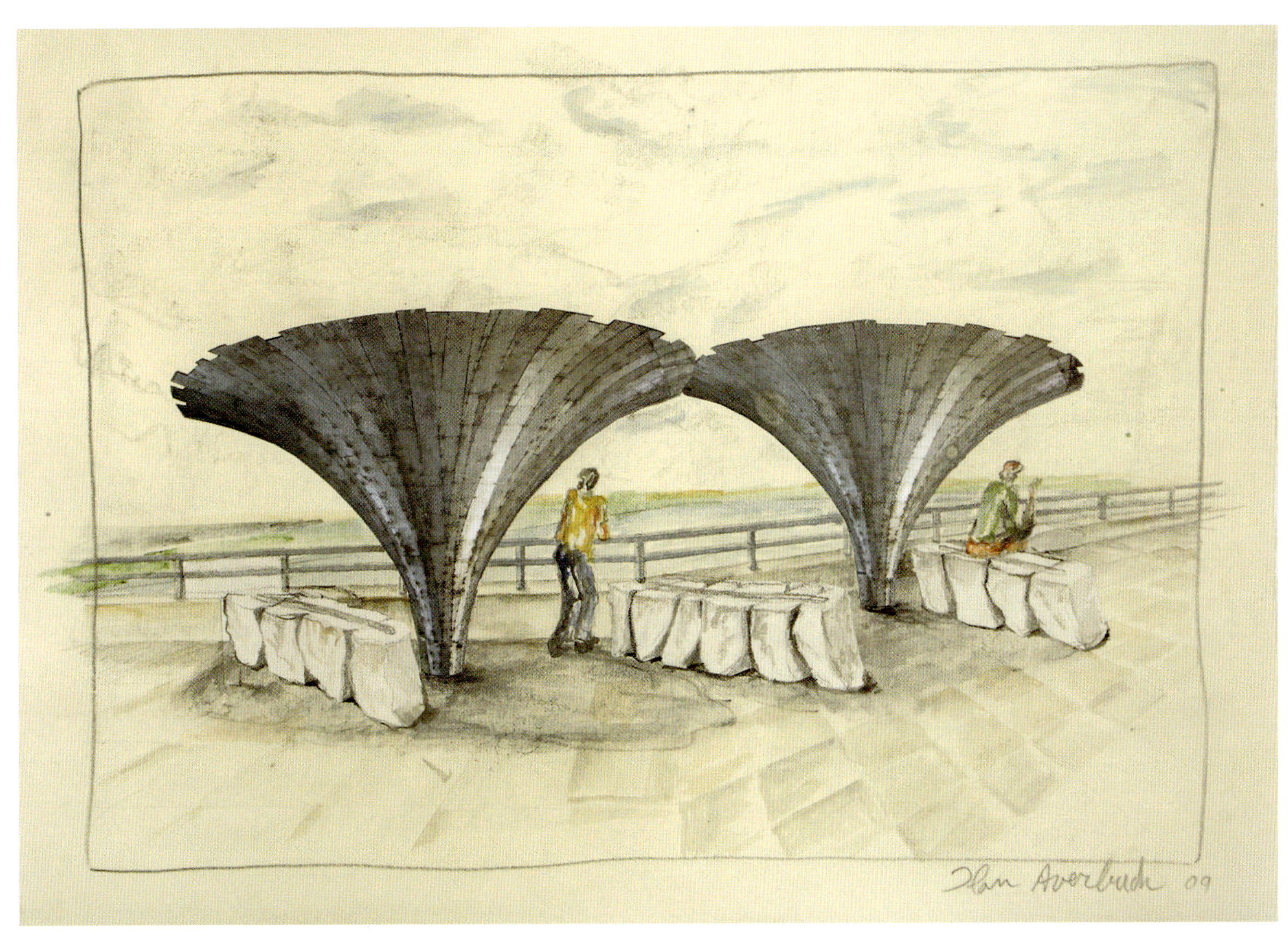

**Water, the Garden of Earth and Sky**, 2009
Mixed media on paper
17 x 24 inches

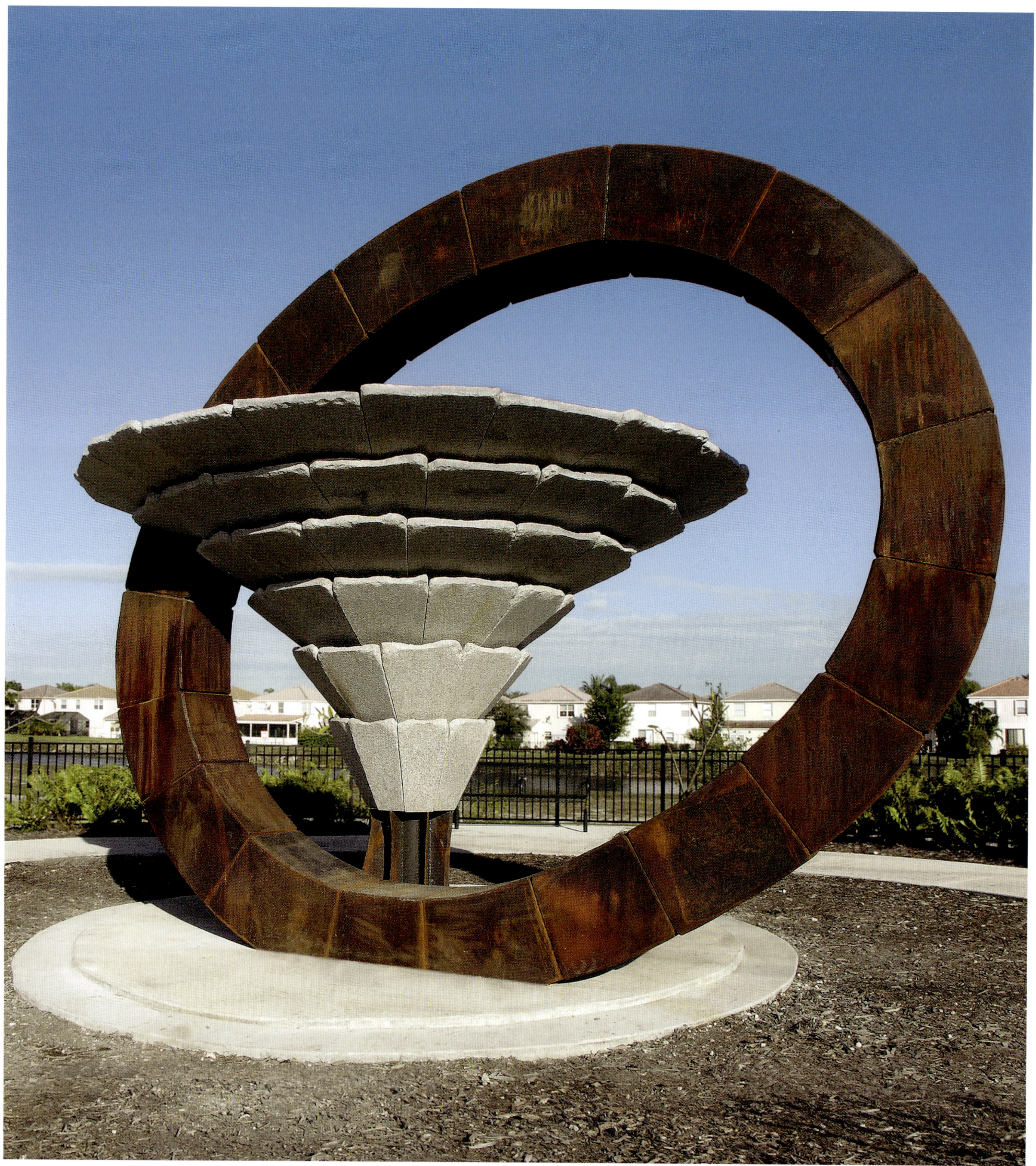

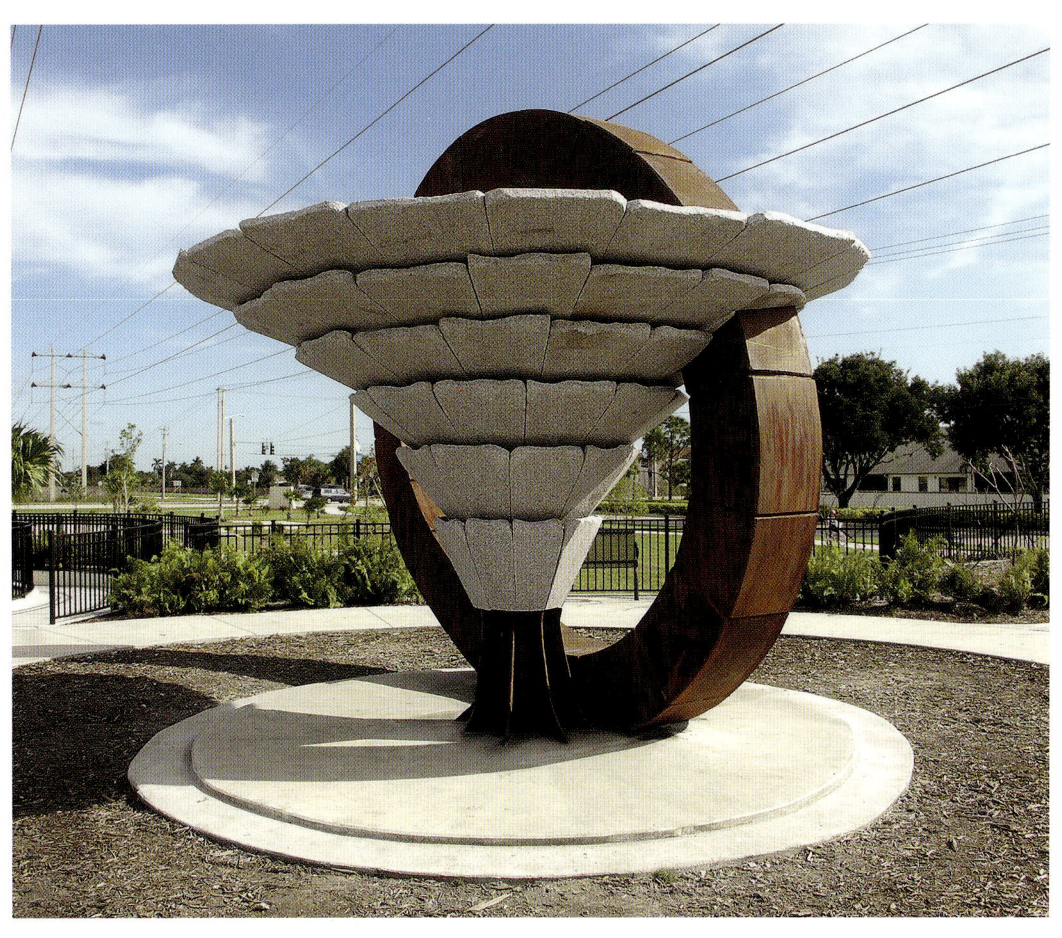

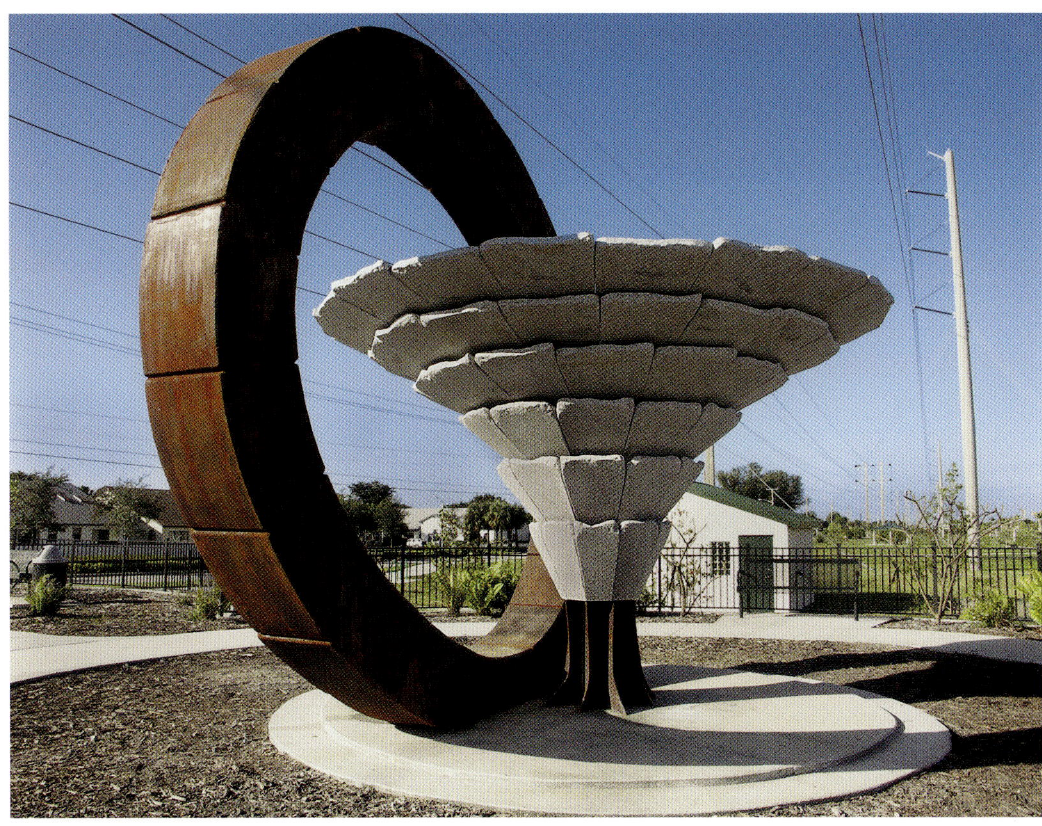

**Under the Shadow of a Big Tree**, 2009
Stone, steel
14 x 18 x 14 feet
Tephford Park, Tamarac, Florida
Commissioned by the City of Tamarac

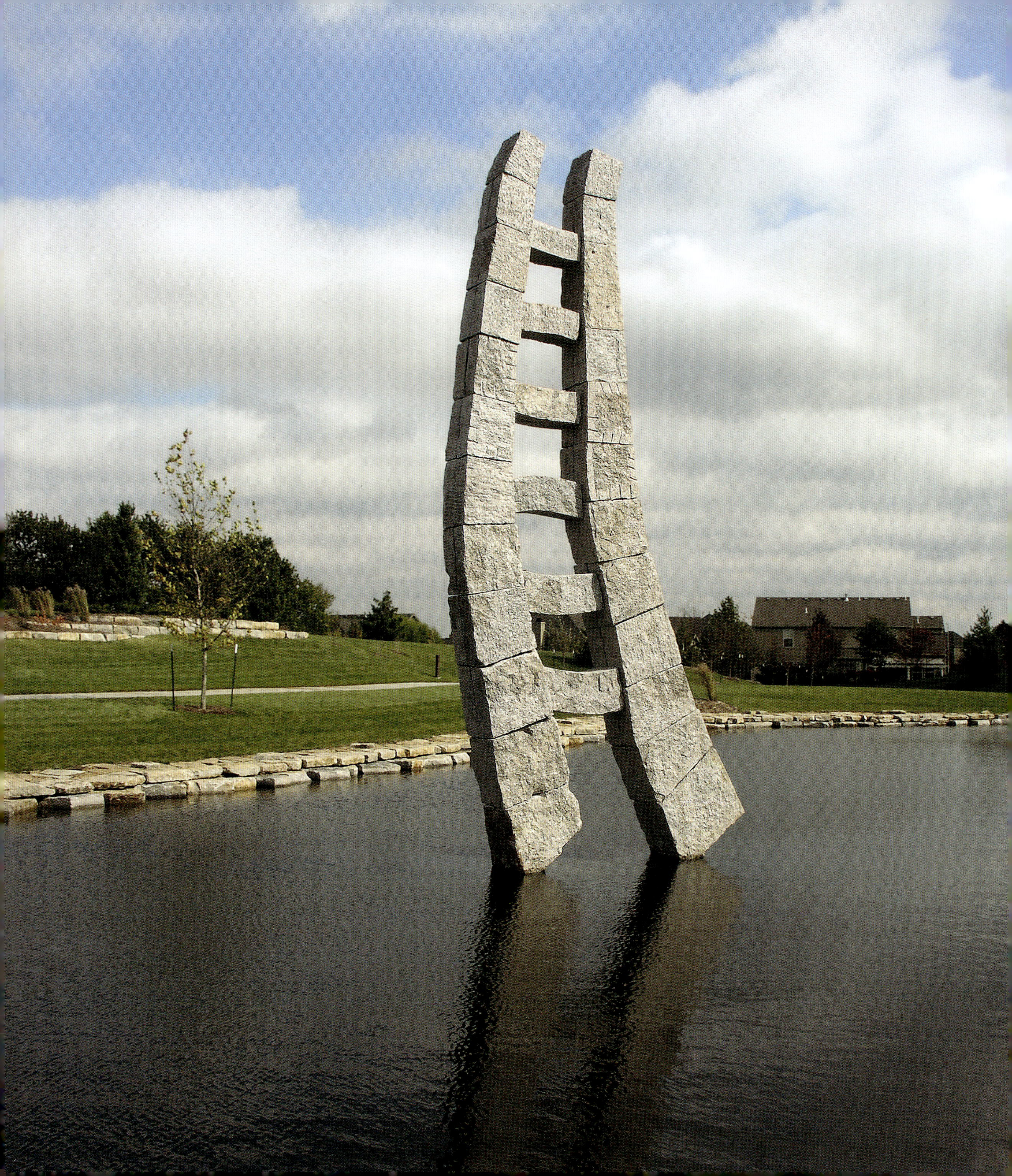

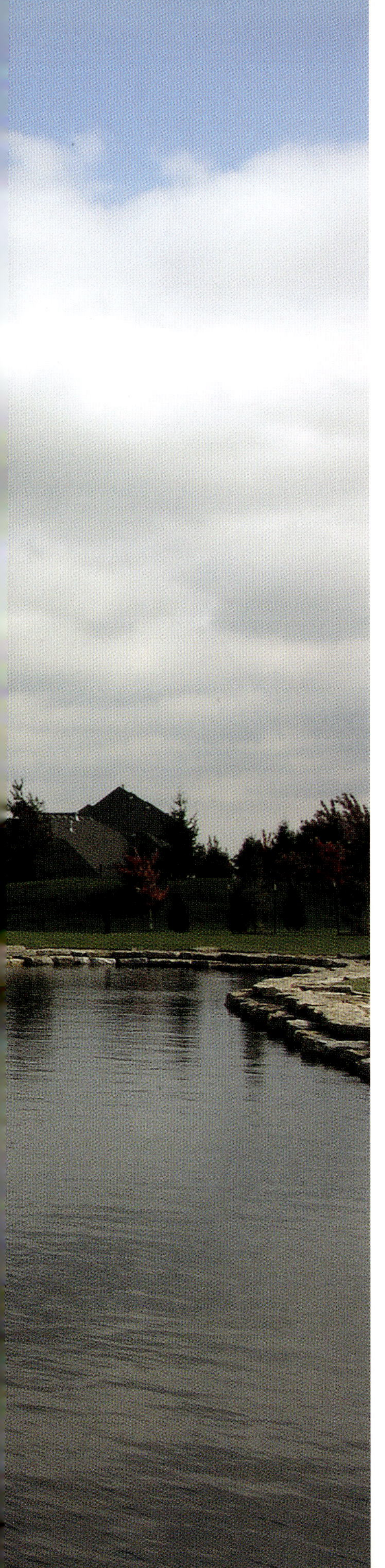

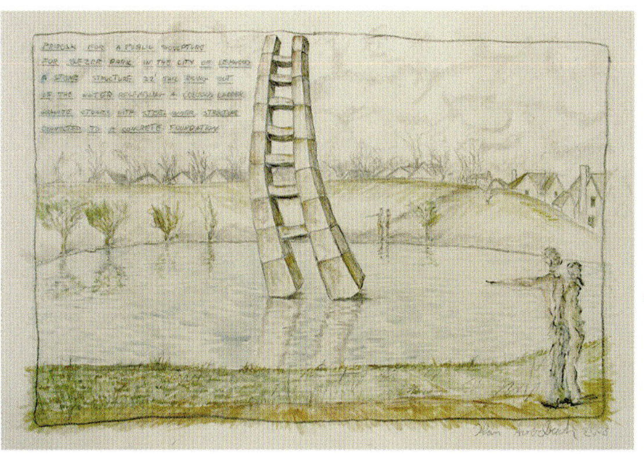

**Avanim Vetseadim (Stones and Steps),** 2008
Stone, steel
24 x 9 1/2 x 2 feet
Gezer Park, Leawood, Kansas
Commissioned by the City of Leawood

**Drawing for Avanim Vetseadim,** 2006
Mixed media on paper
30 x 44 inches

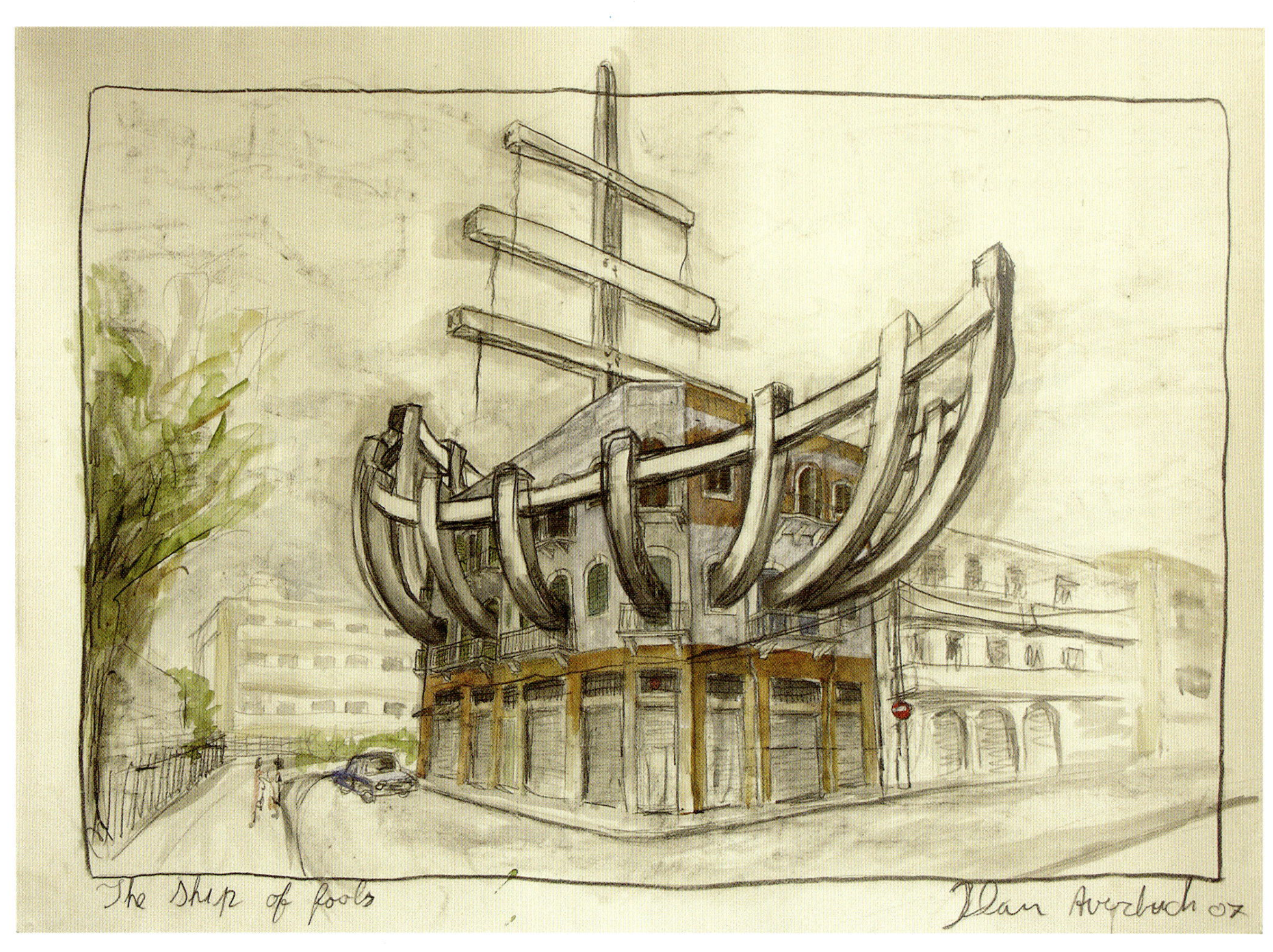


**Ship of Fools**, 2007
Mixed media on paper
30 x 44 inches
Collection of Claudio and Mariapia Basilico

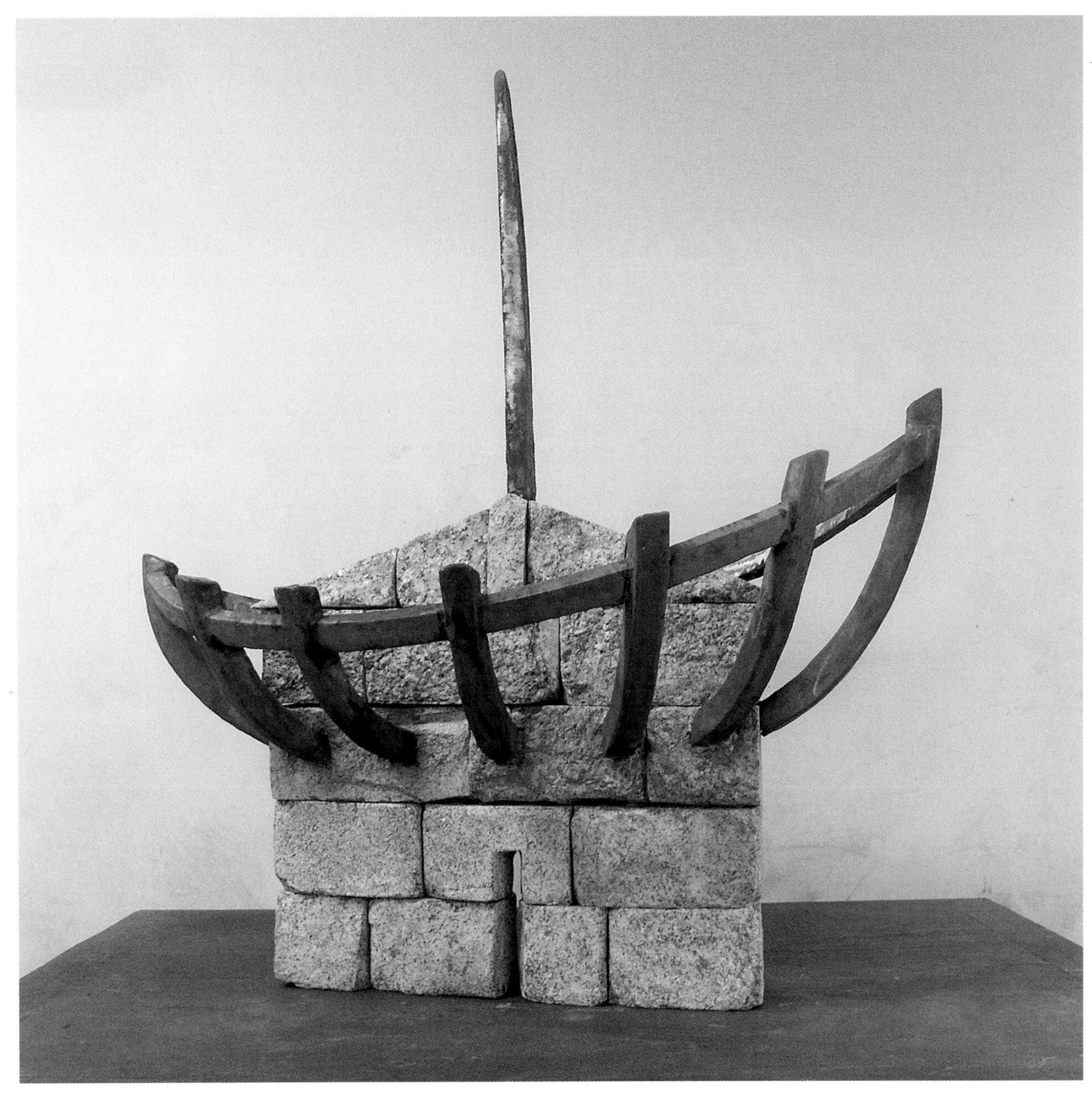

**Ship of Fools**, model in development, 2009
Stone, steel
50 x 45 x 26 inches

# PUBLIC PROJECTS AND WORKS IN PUBLIC
## ILAN AVERBUCH

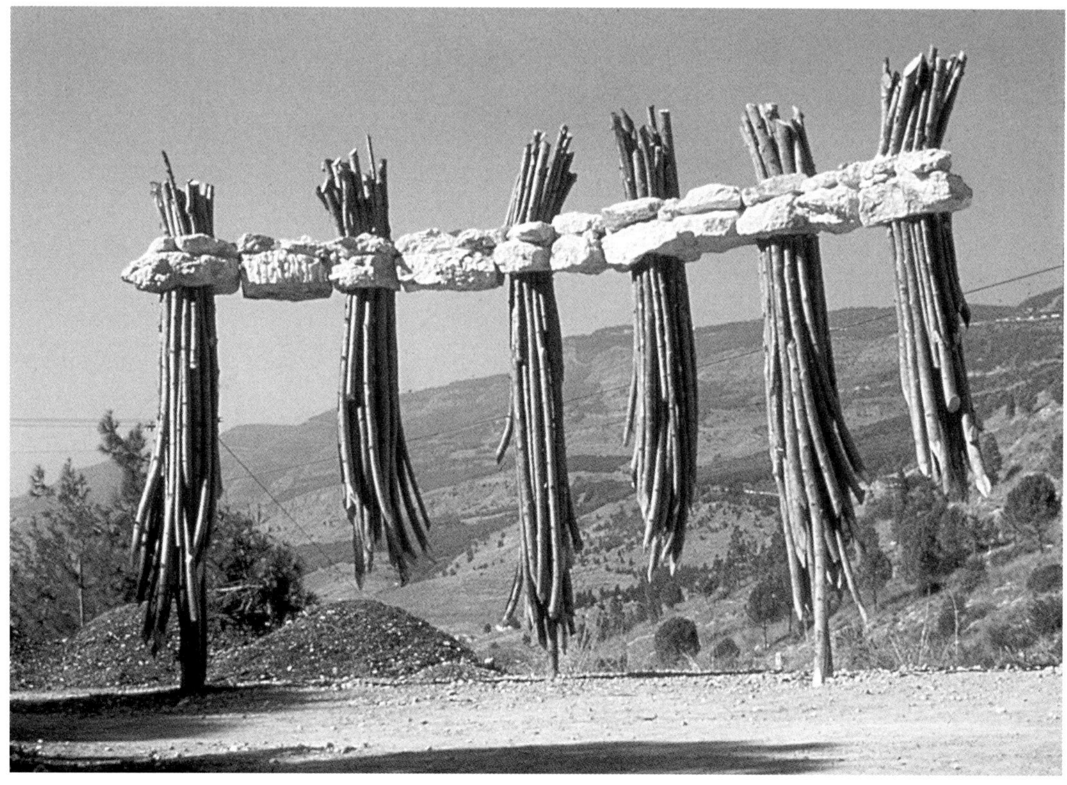

**Tel Hai**, 1983
Wood, stone, steel, earth
12 x 40 x 20 feet
Tel Hai, Israel

What is a public project? This is one of the many questions I found myself asking when I set out to assemble this book. My works in galleries and museums over the past twenty-five years are well documented in reviews, catalogues, magazine ads, and the galleries themselves, where they have a constant home for viewing. After the exhibit is packed up, the works live on and are documented in images. But my public projects are different: they do not have a single place or home where they can be seen. Although in my mind they form a single narrative that evolves from one work to the next, it is difficult for the average art lover to appreciate them. They are located in faraway places, and to see them all you would have to travel to India, Israel, Europe, Canada, and many parts of the USA—no small task.

The term "public project" usually refers to the intention, funding, and administrative process for designing and fabricating the work, such as the Percent for Art and Art in Architecture programs. While many of my sculptures have ended up in public places, not all of them followed the traditional route of getting there. Some of them were originally designed for private venues but somehow wound up in the public realm. Others were conceived as public projects but did not get commissioned: I could not bear to stash the ideas in a drawer, so I went ahead, built them with my own funds, and exhibited them. Did they cease to be public projects as a result?

Let me try to explain the public dimension that so much of my work has almost inevitably acquired. This destiny stems in part from the medium of sculpture, in part from my attraction to a large scale, and in part from my choice of materials. I started making large sculptures while I was still at school, also because of what I had done and where I had been before I made the decision to become an artist. In 1976–1977 I traveled for a long period, close to two years, in North and mostly South America. I lived between the Cordilleras and the Amazon region for long periods, breathing the Incan and Mayan sites, or searching for tribal people and their life deep in the Amazon, where art and life are one. I was actually searching for myself and what I should become. The answer, "art," had a different scale to it. It was a direct translation of what I was going through and a way of replacing these experiences with the fabrication of things, of searching for meaning in the building of objects and environments.

I studied art in London and New York in the late 1970s and early 1980s, after the heyday of minimalism but still very much under its influence. Artists like Smithson, Christo, and Serra were the talk of the town. For me, scale came as a natural progression. At the same time it forced the question, "What do you do with this mammoth creation?" Many of the post-minimalist artists worked subversively, not showing the work itself, but only photographs and other documentation of it. I did not share this method; I wanted to build it and enable it to exist in real spaces. I pushed the scale of my works to the dimensions of the large SoHo galleries, but I always thought bigger.

Once I had completed my first degree in art and had my first round of exhibitions in the early 1980s, I returned to my old habits and traveled to the vast subcontinent of South Asia, to India and Nepal, to recharge myself and my art-making for another long period. When I came back, I channeled the experience into my next few years of work, exhibitions, and subsequent public sculptures.

Israel, where I grew up before these travels and art studies began, was a young country embroiled in wars and the struggle to create a nation out of immigrants from half the world who had arrived only a few years earlier from devastating experiences. The making of a nation was often celebrated in grand-scale monuments, etched into our psyche as milestones in the life of a nation. Every war and every victory was celebrated by a harvest of new monuments by gifted young artists who had learned their craft in Paris, London, or Berlin, at the Beaux-Arts or the Bauhaus. The art market's number one collector was the state, and the birth of a nation the subject matter. In the 1960s this approach combined with the emerging zeitgeist of individualism to produce a new hybrid of art with large subject matter and personal style.

Israel is layered with historic remains, and everywhere you look there are archeological sites. I resisted the nationalistic politics inherent to digging into the remote past for answers, but I nevertheless adopted the methodology of using fragments, lost narratives, and poetic interpretations (as in archeology) to drive my aesthetics.

My first venture into public space was in 1983 in Tel Hai, in the northern part of Israel, not far from the heavily contested border with Lebanon. I was living and showing in New York at the time, and had been invited to take part in an exhibition with major figures who worked in public spaces, such as Jochen Gerz and Dennis Oppenheim. Questions of location, the great landscape, and identity needed to be addressed, as did the possibilities offered by local materials. A few years later I received my first official public project from the city of Tel Aviv, *Harp the Sea and the Quiet Wind*. In addition to designing and executing the work, I also played a large role in choosing the site, which has the open sea on one side and a direct view of an old Islamic minaret on the other. It is also on the demarcation line between Tel Aviv, the new Jewish city, and Jaffa, the old Arabic city, rooted in centuries gone by. The sculptural form I created alluded to a harp (the biblical instrument), but it was made of massive stones, with burnt wooden beams as the mute strings.

An invitation from Berlin in 1986 to build a piece in commemoration of the city's 750th anniversary yielded a work using recycled railroad ties rising up from the real tracks and supporting rows of pavement stones in the air. The stones had been discarded after the devastation of the Second World War. Titled *Wheat in Berlin*, this work evokes the silhouettes of figures marching down the tracks. The displacement echoed in the materials and structure and the irony in the title make it impossible to escape the tension between the recent history of the place and the painterly sculpture I had created.

Back in New York I was discovering my outdoor scale through a work in Socrates Sculpture Park titled *Songs of Love and Hate*. The park, created by Mark di-Suvero, one of the largest-scale outdoor sculptors, overlooks the East River with the Manhattan skyline as a backdrop. When Mark saw the work, he commented that it reminded him of Ingmar Bergman, the Swedish filmmaker. In fact, cinema has had a tremendous effect on my generation of sculptors. I was flattered by his observation, since I have always been interested in the way image, forces of dislocation, and shift of scale play with the viewer's mindset, devices that Bergman often used in his existential meditations on mortality, loneliness, and faith.

A new direction in my sculpture grew out of a competition in Frankfurt in 1988, for which I proposed the image of a toppled dome as a memorial to a synagogue that had stood in the same plaza before the Nazis came to power. I did not get the commission, but for the next few years I built many works with that image in mind. Two ended up in a sculpture park near San Francisco, another in Germany, one in the south of Israel, and the last, *She Wolf*, at Brock University in Canada.

The fallen object and the shift in scale reemerged in Portland, Oregon, in one of my largest and most complex public works. The sculpture was supposed to be situated between the basketball arena and the coliseum. I opted instead to build three objects, each marking a different entrance to the complex, each in a different style and mood, each with a different set of materials.

The continued search for durable and expressive materials led to one of my most interesting experiences. In 1995 I traveled to India with an invitation to work in Calcutta. I was hoping to work in the foundries dotting the area after years of being fascinated by the cast-iron manhole covers in the streets of New York City, many of which bear the imprint, "Made in India." In the few months

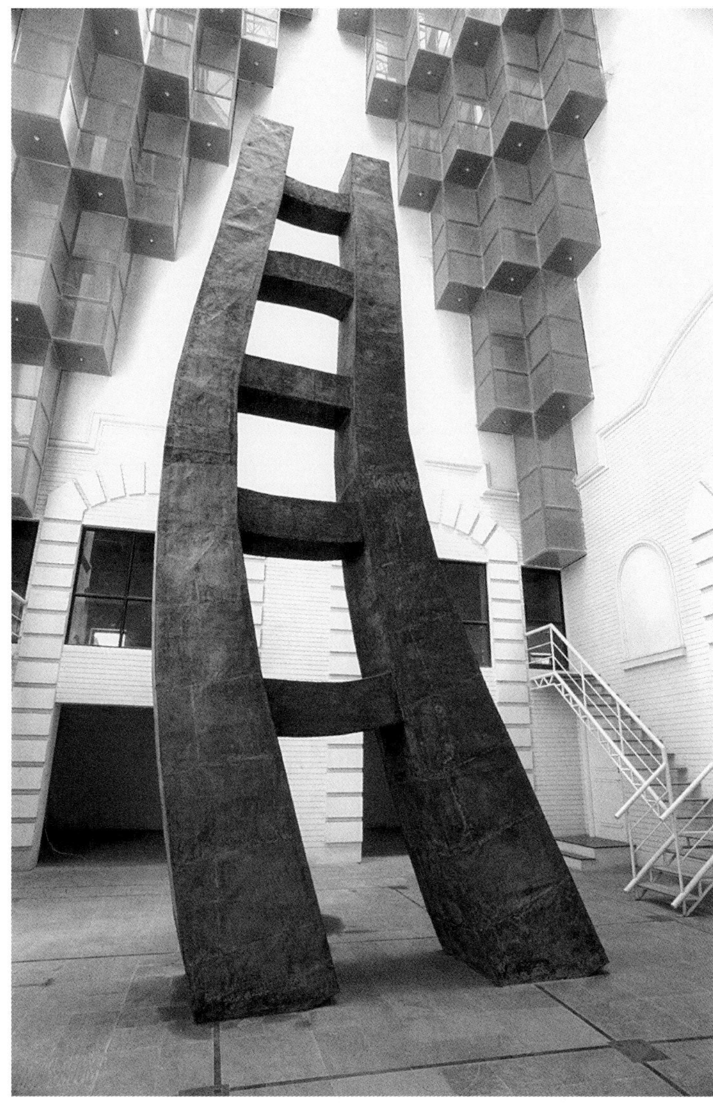

**Calcutta Ladder**, 1998
Copper
28 x 10 x 4 feet
Collection of Ganapati Corporation,
Calcutta, India

I spent at these infernos, I produced several large works in cast iron. *The River* ended up at the Open Museum in Tefen, Israel. Another piece ended up in Calcutta, and a monumental project called *Calcutta Ladder*, rising 28 feet inside an interior atrium, was built in copper for a corporation in Calcutta. Most of the time my travels lead to ideas that I work out in my studio and install at another location, thus twice removed from the place that inspired them. With the *Ladder*, instead, there was a fusion of subject matter, fabrication, setting of the finished work, and geographic source of the original inspiration.

Thanks to an extensive mid-career show in 1997 at the Open Museum, many of my sculptures became permanent fixtures in the beautiful setting of the Galilee, ending years of their wandering among different European cities and venues. The Museum also commissioned me to build a work at the entrance to the town of Lavon, one of their satellite projects. The result, *Divided World*, was the first time I had used distance, the computer, and the digital camera to work out my political and intellectual beliefs. Until then I had either built everything myself or directly supervised its construction. For *Divided World*, instead, I deliberately subcontracted the various parts to different groups. The casting was done at a foundry in central Israel filled with new Jewish immigrants from the former Soviet Union. The stone work, using recycled local stones, was done by local Arabs according to their age-old methods and skills. Back in New York every morning I received pictures on my computer of the previous day's work, and I conveyed my comments to their cell phones or computers from the protection of my studio. I needed the thousands of miles between New York and The Galilee to be able to communicate with both sides, since the distance made them equal to each other and made me equal to them. This structure was the essence of my feelings and thoughts, and I was creating it for one of the most idyllic, politically volatile,

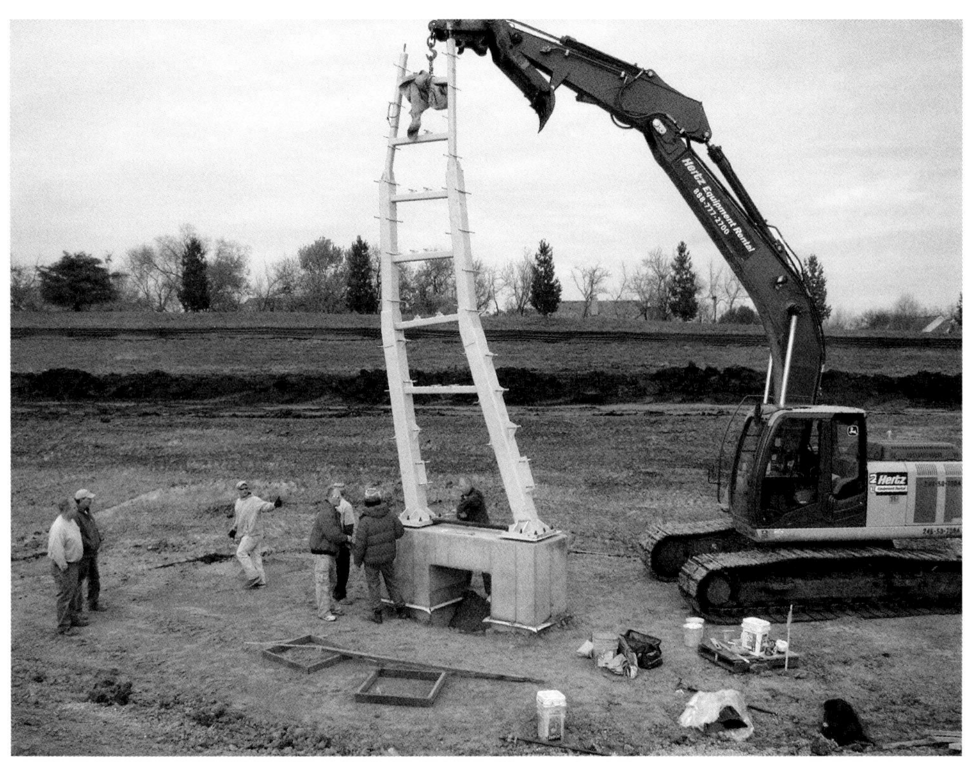

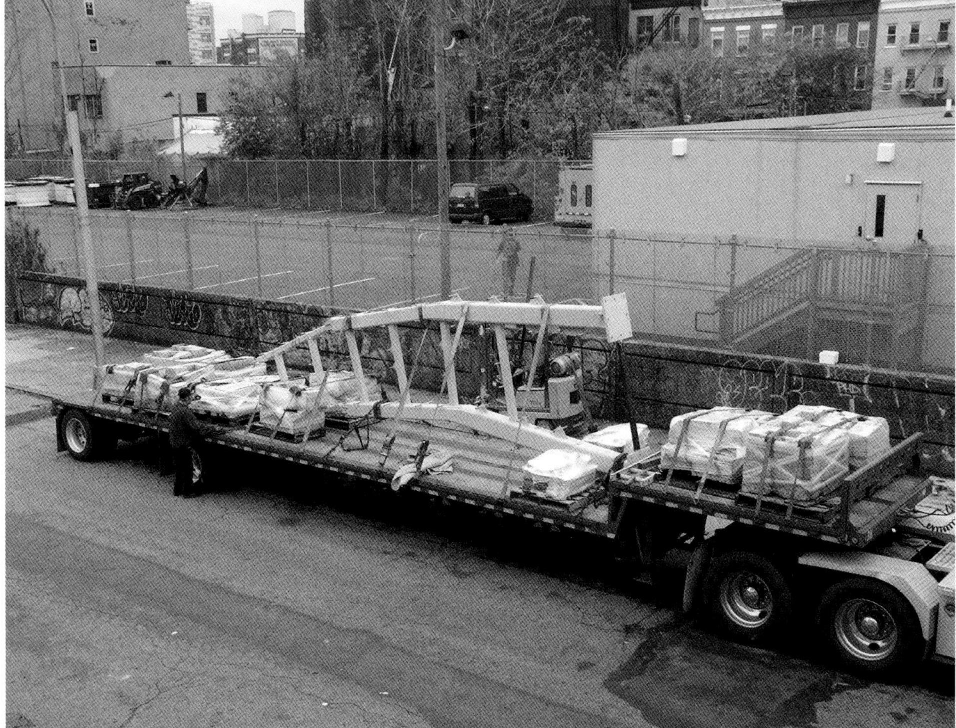

Raising the structure
Sculputure ready for shipment

and cherished places I know. It was also the moment when I felt my public work come to maturity.

Many of the public works I have completed since that crucial moment have brought their own criteria and challenges. Each has demanded a deep meditation on a place and its unique set of problems, colors, temperature, and history. At the same time, a whole host of personal issues accompany me to the drawing board: where I am, or what I am experiencing at that juncture in my life and work. With *Dove Tower and Steps to the Bottom of a Pyramid* (2004) I was searching for the moment of precise balance between a towering, leaning columbarium and the serenity of an upside-down pyramid buried in the ground. It serves as a place of meditative calm in the isolation below ground level, but it is also under the shadow of the precarious upside-down tower. These were also the years after September 11, an event that unintentionally found its way into the work.

There may be no better example of the complexity of my public projects than *Avanim Vetseadim (Stones and Steps)* (2008–2009) in Leawood, Kansas. It is situated in a new park with a natural water source turned into a beautiful pond. I reworked the image of a giant ladder that I had previously made in copper for an indoor setting in Calcutta. This time it became a massive 24-foot-tall stone sculpture made of recycled stones from a bridge in Pennsylvania. The sturdy construction of roughly carved granite bends and twists as if it were a figure tip-toeing across the surface of the pond. Through its ever-changing reflection in the water, the image doubles in size. We expect a ladder to be sturdily planted on the ground. Here, instead, we find the mirror image of the top where we expect the bottom to be, making the ladder look as if it were floating in mid-air.

Questions of time and space, image and form, gravity and weightlessness, movement and stasis all come together to choreograph the whole environment into a single work of art. Because of the nature of the venue for which it was created—the public arena—it will probably outlast all of us, you and me alike, and generations to come will interpret and live with it.

APPENDIX

# ILAN AVERBUCH
## BIOGRAPHY

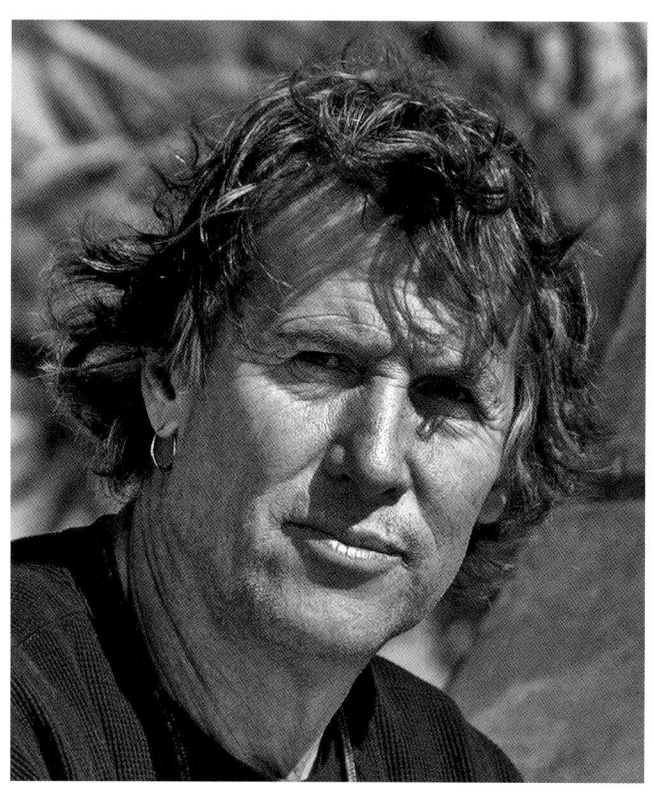

Born in Tel Aviv, Israel.
Currently lives and works in New York and Tel Aviv.
**www.ilanaverbuch.com**


EDUCATION:
1983–1985
Hunter College, New York, New York, M.F.A.

1979–1981
School of Visual Arts, New York, New York, B.F.A.

1977–1978
Wimbledon School of Art, London, England


SELECTED COMMISSIONS:
2010
**Scottsdale, Arizona:** Eldorado Fire Station
**Harriman, Salt Lake County, Utah:**
A large-scale sculpture between the Sorenson
Recreation Center and the library

2009
**Danielson, Connecticut:**
HH Ellis Technical High School
**Tamarac, Florida:** A sculpture in a public park built
to commemorate a fallen police officer
**Salem, Oregon:** A sculpture in four parts on the entry
plaza of the Oregon State Data Center

2008
**Tacoma, Washington:** Major outdoor
sculpture and one smaller sculpture for Sound
Transit light rail system
**Leawood, Kansas:** Large stone work
as a centerpiece of Gezer Park
**Phoenix, Arizona:** Major outdoor sculpture and two
smaller sculptures for new Light Rail System

2007
**Yehud, Israel:** Outdoor sculpture in a prominent public
traffic circle, funded by Mercury Corporation

2006
**Stapleton, Denver, Colorado:** Landmark
as part of the Stapleton urban renewal project
**Tierra Verde, Florida:** Outdoor sculpture
for Tierra Verde Fire Station #2

2004
**Storrs, Connecticut:** University
of Connecticut: Major outdoor sculpture
for the IT and Engineering Building

2003
**Ramat-Gan, Israel:** An outdoor sculpture
for a plaza and gathering area at Bar-Ilan University
**Naharia, Israel:** Meidatech Corporation

2002
**Phoenix, Arizona:** Design Committee
for six stations of the new light rail system
**Chulon, Israel:** The Little Prince Park, Chulon, Israel

2001
**Peoria, Illinois:** Large outdoor work in front of the
Performing Arts Center at Illinois Central College

2000
**Lavon, Israel:** Landmark work at the entrance to the town

1996
**Ganapati Inc., Calcutta, India:** Sculpture
in the atrium of corporate office building

1995
**Portland, Oregon:** Three sculptures, one at each
entrance to the Rose Garden Arena complex

1989
**City of Tel Aviv, Israel:** Sculpture at the edge of the sea


SELECT SOLO EXHIBITIONS:
**Nancy Hoffman Gallery**, New York, New York:
2008, 2005, 2002, 1999, 1997, 1995, 1993, 1991, 1989
**Olga Korper Gallery**, Toronto, Canada:
2009, 2005, 1998, 1994, 1991, 1988
**Katonah Museum of Art**, Katonah, New York: 2005
**Galerie Sander**, Darmstadt, Germany: 2001
**Künstverein Hürth**, Hürth, Germany: 2000
**Köln Art Fair, Galerie Lutz Teutloff**, Köln, Germany: 1999
**Galerie Lutz Teutloff**, Bielefeld and Köln, Germany:
1998, 1996, 1993
**Michael Haas Gallery**, Berlin, Germany: 1993, 1990, 1987
**The Open Museum**, Tefen, Israel: 1997
**Littmann Gallery**, Basel, Switzerland: 1994
**Julie M. Gallery**, Tel Aviv, Israel: 1997, 1993
**Het Apollohuis**, Eindhoven, The Netherlands: 1992
**Lavignes-Bastille**, Paris, France: 1990
**The Jewish Museum**, New York, New York: 1986
**Mabat Gallery**, Tel Aviv, Israel: 1986
**DAAD Galerie**, Berlin, Germany: 1986.
**Künstlerhaus Bethanien**, Berlin, Germany: 1985
**OK Harris Works of Art**, New York, New York:
1987, 1985, 1983, 1981
**List Art Center**, Brown University, Providence,
Rhode Island: 1983

SELECT GROUP EXHIBITIONS:
2004
**Museum Opening Exhibition**, Nevada Art Museum, Reno, Nevada
*Indivisible Cities*, Bill Maynes Gallery, New York, New York

2003
*Shivat Zion, Beyond the Principle of Place*, Zman Leomanut, Israel
*Givataim Connection*, Israel
*Genetic Expressions: Art After DNA*, Heckscher Museum of Art, New York, New York
*Grand Opening of the New Nevada Museum of Art*, Reno, Nevada

2002
*Markers II*, Kassel, Germany
*Hands*, Israel Museum, Jerusalem, Isreal

2001
**DeCordova Museum and Sculpture Park**, Lincoln, Massachusetts
**Galerie Sander at the Berlin Art Fair**, Berlin, Germany

1999
*The Hand*, The Power Plant, Toronto, Canada
*Food for Thought*, New Jersey Center for Visual Arts, Summit, New Jersey

1997
"Pier Walk '97", Navy Pier, Chicago, Illinois

1996–1997
Socrates Sculpture Park, Long Island City, New York

1994
**Basel Art Fair**, Switzerland
*Kunstwert*, Berlin, Germany

1993
*New York Diary: Almost 25 Different Things*, P.S. 1 Museum, Long Island City, New York
*Sticks and Stones: 10 Artists Work with Nature*, Katonah Museum of Art, Katonah, New York

1990
*Construction in Process*, Lodz, Poland Historical Museum, Lodz, Poland
*A Natural Order*, Hudson River Museum, Yonkers, New York

1989
*Recent Acquisitions*, Art Gallery of Ontario, Toronto, Canada
**Socrates Park**, Astoria, Queens, New York
*Recent Acquisitions*, Tel Aviv Museum, Israel

1988
**Bronfman Centre**, Montreal, Canada
**The Brooklyn Museum**, Brooklyn, New York

1987
*Mythos Berlin*, Anhalter Bahnhof, Berlin, Germany

1985
**The Peace Biennale**, Hamburg, Germany

1984
*80 Years of Israeli Sculpture*, Israel Museum, Jerusalem, Israel

1983
**Tel Hai '83**, Tel Hai Art Center, Israel


SELECT AWARDS AND GRANTS:
2001
**Pollock-Krasner Foundation Grant**

1991
**Mid-Atlantic Art Award**, NEA regional fellowship
**D.A.A.D. Award**, Berlin, Germany


SELECT COLLECTIONS:
**Bronfman Centre for the Arts**, Montreal, Canada
**Michael Haas**, Berlin, Germany
**Christopher Horn**, Toronto, Canada
**Israel Museum**, Jerusalem, Israel
**Estate of Eugene Klein**, California
**Martin Margulies**, Florida International University, Miami, Florida
**Prudential Insurance Company**, Ltd., Newark, New Jersey
**Runnymede Sculpture Farm**, Woodside, California
**Yochen Sander**, Darmstadt, Germany
**The Open Museum**, Industrial Park, Tefen, Israel
**Tel Aviv Museum of Art**, Israel
**Telesat**, Ottawa, Canada
**Tel Hai Art Center**, Israel
**Tel Noff Sculpture Garden**, Israel
**Manfred Kronen**, Düsseldorf, Germany
**Lutz Teutloff**, Bielefeld, Germany
**Harsh Neotia**, Calcutta, India
**Ed Bazinet**, St. Paul, Minnesota
**Robert Duncan**, Lincoln, Nebraska
**Stefan Janssen**, Carefree, Arizona

John Schmid, Basel, Switzerland
Danny Avlas, Herzliya, Israel
Hava Gal-On, Ramat Hasharon, Israel
Nevada Museum of Art, Reno
Martin and Joan Messinger, Harrison, New York
Robert Davoli and Eileen Mcdonagh, Lincoln,
Massachusetts
Brock Seymour/A1 Label Corporation, Toronto,
Canada


SELECT CATALOGUES:
(*indicates solo show catalogues)

*Ilan Averbuch: Das Gelobte Land.
Kunstverein Hürth, Hürth, Germany. 2000.

*Ilan Averbuch, Sculpture and Drawing.
The Open Museum, Tefen, Israel.
Essays: "Ilan Averbuch: The Intimate Monument,"
Carter Ratcliff; "Upon Thy Places and Times,"
Dr. Gideon Ofrat. 1997.

*Ilan Averbuch Sculpturen Zeichnugen.
Galerie Michael Haas, Berlin,
and Lutz Teutloff Modern Art, Köln. 1993.

Sticks and Stones, Katonah Museum of Art,
New York. 1991.

Israel Contemporary Sculpture:
place and mainstream. Hara Museum,
Japan. 1991.

Mid-Atlantic Arts Foundation, NEA,
Regional Fellowships. 1991.

*Ilan Averbuch.
Galerie Michael Haas-Berlin,
Nancy Hoffman Gallery-New York,
Olga Korper Gallery-Toronto, Lavignes-Bastille-Paris.
Essay: "The Monumental Archaeologue:
Ilan Averbuch's Sculpture," Donald Kuspit. 1990.

A Natural Order, The Hudson River Museum,
New York. 1990.

40 From Israel, Contemporary Sculpture and Drawing.
Brooklyn Museum, Brooklyn, New York. 1988.

Fresh Paint. Tel Aviv Museum and Israel Museum,
Isreal. 1988.

Mythos Berlin Project, Berlin, West Germany. 1987.

*Averbuch. DAAD Galerie, Berlin, Germany.
Essay: "Ilan Averbuch," Donald Kuspit. 1986.

Contemporary Sculpture from the Martin Z. Marguiles
Collection, Grove Isle, Coconut Grove, Florida.
Introduction: Paula Harper. 1986.

Biennale Des Friedens. Künsthaus und Künstverein,
Hamburg, Germany. 1985.

Israel Art. Israel Museum, Jerusalem,
Isreal. 1985.

Tel Hai 83. Contemporary Art Meeting,
Israel. 1983.

Philadelphia Tricentennial Show. 1982.

To find out more about Charta,
and to learn about our most recent publications, visit

**www.chartaartbooks.it**

Printed in May 2010
by arti grafiche BIANCA&VOLTA, Truccazzano,
for Edizioni Charta